Library of
Davidson College

TOP MANAGEMENT CONTROL IN EUROPE

Top Management Control in Europe

JACQUES HENRI HOROVITZ

St. Martin's Press
New York

© Jacques Henri Horovitz 1980

All rights reserved. For information write:
St. Martin's Press Inc., 175 Fifth Avenue, New York, N.Y. 10010
Printed in Hong Kong
First published in the United States of America in 1980

ISBN 0–312–80908–5
LCN 79–25238

To my wife Annette

Contents

List of Tables xii

List of Figures xv

Acknowledgments xvii

Introduction 1
   The Issue 1
   Scope of the Study 3
   Organisation of the Book 4

Part One Setting the Stage 7

1 Comparative Management: The Current State of the Art 9
   Scope of Chapter 9
   Comparative Management: Objectives and Scope of the
      Field 9
   Critical Issues in Comparative Management 11
      The Universality Issue 12
      The Missing Link between Comparative
         Management and Existing Management Theories 15
      The Need for Process-Oriented Studies 16
   Implications for this Research 17
   Summary 18

2 Management Control and Associated Variables 23
   Scope of Chapter 23
   Strategy of Research 23
   Control and Controls 24

Independent Variables Investigated	30
Business Variables	30
Management System Variables	33
Country Variables	34
Summary	35

3 Research Design and Methodology   38

Scope of Chapter	38
Basic Research Design	38
Choice of Industry Sectors and Companies	40
Criteria for Choosing Industries	40
Practical Choice of Industries	40
Practical Choice of Potential Sample Firms	41
Data Collection	43
Persons Interviewed	43
Highlights on the Data Collection Tools Used	45
Summary	49

Part Two Describing Cross National Differences and Similarities   51

4 Management Processes: Structure and Planning   53

Scope of Chapter	53
The Process of Organising	54
Highlight on Basic Management Structure: an Overall Comparative View	54
The Basic Division of Labour	55
Division of Labour within the Top Management Team	63
Central Staff and Span of Control	65
Delegation of Authority and Decentralisation of Decision-Making	66
Committee Management	67
Summary	69
The Corporate Long-Range Planning Process	70
Highlights of Findings: a Comparative View	70
The Use of Corporate Long-Range Planning	71
The Organisation of Planning	72
Planning Content	72
The Planning Process	75
Summary	78

Contents ix

5 Management Control: the Chief Executive's Viewpoint	80
Management Control Objectives Pursued by Chief Executives	80
Control as a Means of ensuring that Performance is as near as Practical to Plan	81
Control as a Policing Device for Operations	83
Control as a Means for Motivation and Inducement of Behaviour	86
Who is in Control in the Organisation	87
Control Intensity over Functions of the Firm	89
Content Frequency and Provision of Top Managers' Reports	93
Overall Comparative View of Findings	93
Content of Reports to Chief Executives	94
Frequency and Degree of Detail	95
Characteristics of Information Supplied to Chief Executives	98
How do they Get those Reports?	99
Some Indications of Top Management Control Effectiveness	101
Summary	102
6 Top Management – the Controllership Function	105
Scope of Chapter	105
Controllers' Objectives Pursued in Control	106
The Functions of Control Departments: their Location, Size and Human Resources	107
In Great Britain: a Heavy Dotted Line	108
In Germany: Move from *Kontrolle* to Controlling	108
The Controller in France: Two Roles	112
Some Elements of Control Costs	112
The Data Base: Cost and Profit Accounting: Emphasis on Reporting to Top Management	114
Cost Accounting and Cost Centres	115
'Profit Accounting' and Profit Centres	116
Short-Range Planning and Control	121
Content and Cycle	122
The Influence of the Controller	123
Summary	124

Contents

7 Operational Control: Marketing and Production	126
Scope of Chapter	126
The Basic Objectives Pursued in Operational Control	126
The Essential Characteristics of Control and the Resulting Degree of Formalism in Operations Control	129
'Tightness of Grasp': a Comparative View of the Control Process	132
The Marketing Control Process: Standard Setting, Measurement and Evaluation of Performance	133
The Production Control Process: Standard Setting, Measurement of Performance and Evaluation	138
Conclusion: Some Indications of Operational Control Effectiveness	141
Summary	142
Part Three Analysing Management Control Practices	145
8 Influences Contributing to Differences in Control Practices between Countries	147
Scope of Chapter	147
Summary of Country Differences in Control Practices within their Contextual (Structure and Planning) Framework	147
Secondary Support for Treating Country Differences Seriously	148
Great Britain	149
Germany	153
France	156
Summary	160
9 Emerging Propositions Regarding Differences in Management Control Practices	162
Scope of Chapter	162
Statistical Scanning for Significant Impacts on Control Practices	162
A Model for the Study of Management Control Practices	167

Propositions Suggested for Research ... 170
  The Debate between Universal and Cultural View
    of Management ... 170
  Interdependency of Planning, Organisation
    Structure and Control in each Company's
    Management System ... 173
  Effect of Professionalisation ... 175
  Influence of Technology and Market Stability ... 177
  The Lack of Influence of Strategy on Control and
    the Weak Link with Management Processes ... 178
Suggestions For Related Research ... 180
  The Case of Less Developed Countries ... 180
  The Link of Management Control with
    Leadership and Motivation ... 181
  Control Effectiveness ... 182
Summary ... 182

Conclusion: Some Implications for Managers ... 185

  British Management ... 185
  German Management ... 187
  French Management ... 188

Bibliography ... 191

Index ... 199

List of Tables

3.1	Basic research design	39
3.2	Number of people interviewed	46
4.1	The basic organisation of labour	56
4.2	Division of labour among top executives	64
4.3	Staff and line	65
4.4	Decentralisation scores by country	67
4.5	Frequency of top management committee meetings	67
4.6	Summary of differences and similarities in the structural characteristics present in the three countries	70
4.7	Number of firms engaging in long-range planning	72
4.8	Location of the planning department within the structure	73
4.9	Number of firms for which long-range plans include structure	74
4.10	Number of firms having a planning manual	75
4.11	Approach to long-range planning	75
5.1	Control helps a superior evaluate a subordinate performance for rewards and/or promotion	87
5.2	Whose task is control?	88
5.3	Are all functions of the firm controlled with equal weight?	89
5.4	Number of times British chief executives ranked the five functions in ranks 1, 2, 3, 4 and 5	91
5.5	Number of times German chief executives ranked the five functions in ranks 1, 2, 3, 4 and 5	91
5.6	Number of times French chief executives ranked the five functions in ranks 1, 2, 3, 4 and 5	92
5.7	Number of companies in which the monthly report to the chief executive includes the following items (computed from a content analysis of documents)	96

List of Tables

5.8	Frequency of top manager's information	97
5.9	Number of times looked at	97
5.10	Number of monthly reports to chief executives which include detailed costs	97
5.11	Characteristics of information supplied to chief executives	100
5.12	Who prepares these reports sent to the chief executives?	101
5.13	Average degree of achievement of five most important objectives in last year	102
5.14	Summary of the tendencies of key characteristics differentiating countries with respect to top management control	103
6.1	Differences in views: chief executives and controllers	106
6.2	Organisation of central control department by main tasks	108
6.3	Average number of people working in management control, at headquarters in the marketing, production and finance domains	113
6.4	Which units serve as a base for a cost centres?	115
6.5	Average proportion in the basis for establishing cost centre's objectives	116
6.6	Basis of profit accounting	117
6.7	Number of years companies have had budgets	121
6.8	Who prepares reports on budget results?	123
6.9	Controller's input on budget results sent to unit	124
7.1	Control ensures that *procedures* are carried out, as defined, by subordinates	127
7.2	Control ensures that orders are carried out, as defined, by subordinates	128
7.3	Control's objective is to keep the boss informed of what is going on in the organisation	128
7.4	Characteristics of operational control in each country	131
7.5	Number of times operational and non-operational marketing objectives have been selected in the top five by marketing managers	135
7.6	The treatment of non-operational marketing objectives objectives in control	135
7.7	Time span of marketing performance measurement	136
7.8	Who defines marketing standards?	137
7.9	Who measures marketing performance?	137
7.10	What is included in reports?	138

List of Tables

7.11 Number of times operational and non-operational production objectives have been chosen in the first five — 139
7.12 Setting standards and measuring performance on qualitative non-operational production objectives — 139
7.13 Interval between production control measurements — 140
7.14 Who sets standards? — 140
7.15 Who measures performance? — 140
7.16 Who evaluates? — 141
7.17 Chief executives' subjective assessments of degrees of success in production and marketing control — 142
8.1 Country differences in structure and planning — 148
8.2 Country differences in control practices — 164
9.1 Control indexes — 166
9.2 Indexes for independent variables
9.3 Overall relationships of control practices with country, country, business and management system variables — 168
9.4 The universality issue — 172

List of Figures

1.1	The Farmer-Richman model	11
2.1	Chosen strategy of research	24
2.2	The control process	25
2.3	Five key dimensions to planning	26
2.4	Dimensions of control focused on subject	27
2.5	Variables influencing control	31
2.6	Influence of technology and market change on the type of management design	32
2.7	Business variables	33
2.8	Management system variables	33
2.9	A model for the study of control	35
3.1	Potential and actual range of companies in the three countries	43
4.1	The basic holding structure in Great Britain	56
4.2	The British holding structure with divisional domains	57
4.3	The British holding structure with divisions	58
4.4	The British pure divisional structure	59
4.5	The German functional organisation	60
4.6	The German divisional structure, type A	61
4.7	The German divisional structure, type B	61
4.8	The French functional organisation	62
4.9	The French functional structure, split operational	62
4.10	The French divisional structure	63
4.11	Functional and divisional roles of Volstand members in Germany	64 78
4.12	Simplified example of target-setting in Germany	
5.1	Control does and should ensure that actual performance comes close to plan	81
5.2	An example of an eleven-person cost centre in Germany	85
5.3	Control used as a policing instrument	86

5.4	Control used for motivating and inducing behaviour	86
6.1	Controlling required	110
6.2	Profit centre accountability: division, sales and production departments in the German company	118
6.3	Profit accounting: product and/or market in the Germany company	118
6.4	Reporting system design	120
6.5	The British planning cycle	122
6.6	The German planning cycle	123
7.1	Interfunction comparative degree of formalism in operational control	129
7.2	Intra-country differential degree of formalism in operational control	130
7.3	Inter-country differential degree of formalism in operational control	130
7.4	Degree of grasp in marketing	133
7.5	Degree of grasp in production	133
9.1	Revised model of control	170
9.2	Evolution of planning and control	175

Acknowledgements

In 1969 the French Foundation for Business Education (FNEGE) was created; its first aim was to send about 400 future business educators on various training programmes in the United States. I was part of the group and I was eager to return to share my knowledge of modern management skills. My return, however, was a cultural shock in more than one way. Those US-trained scholars were looked upon defiantly by the old guard, but the biggest shock came from the lack of local data on which to use these freshly-acquired concepts and skills. Was it all right to talk about a model devised in the US after maybe fifteen years of observations of actual behaviour? American teaching material was handy, but did it convey the skills desired and needed by industry? These types of questions puzzled me and I decided to embark on an empirical study of actual management practices in Europe in view of the relative void existing in European material, and this study is a modest contribution to bridge the gap between management principles and actual practices.

Interviewing over 180 executives in 52 medium-size local European companies was both a challenge and a pleasure. These companies are not often visited by academics and in many cases I was looked upon with curiosity. I want to thank all the executives for their time, welcome and cooperation as well as the Confederation of British Industries and l'Union des Industries Metallurgiques et Minières for their assistance.

Comparative research is probably one of the most expensive types of research. This study would not have been possible without a generous grant from the FNEGE and a Samuel Bronfman fellowship for which I am both honoured and grateful.

Besides the costs, comparative research is also one of the most time-consuming and physically demanding ones. During the study I have spent more time on a plane, a train, a car or on the phone than at home. The fact that my father is Russian, my mother Polish and my wife Vietnamese must have given me a certain openness to international research. But, above all, in all these trips and efforts, I would have been easily overcome by a Slavic tendency for despair had it not been for a counterbalancing Asiatic philosophy of fatality. This is why this work is dedicated to my wife Annette.

I am very grateful to Professor William H. Newman of Columbia University who all along provided the precious guidance, comments and advice without which my tendency to grasp all European reality at once would have resulted in chaos.

If I had any doubt about the sense of organisation and exactness which I found in the eighteen German companies visited, Peter Kessler who helped me arrange interviews and translate in Germany must constitute the nineteenth case.

To all my deepest appreciation and thanks.

Paris, December 1978   JACQUES H. HOROVITZ

Introduction

THE ISSUE

Comparative management continues to be an area calling for exploration. In fact, authors who advance the view that management is culture-bound have been contradicted by both the defendants of the 'universal' approach to management – implying the cross-border transferability of management principles – and the defendants of the 'individualistic' approach implying that management basically is a personal matter.

Resolution of these diverging views has theoretical importance for the conceptualisation of the way social organisations are guided. It also has practical significance for attempts to transfer managerial 'know-how' from one country to another, and for multinational companies that must coordinate operations among several different countries.

This study presents data directly related to the core of this comparative management debate. It reports on an exploratory, in-depth study focused on management practices in three countries – France, England and Germany. Although the literature on comparative management is rapidly expanding, most of it deals either with multinational companies or with separate studies in individual countries. The few empirical cross-countries studies have dealt with a single factor such as origins of managerial elites, or they make comparisons on a gross basis. The present study moves into the remaining gap of direct comparisons of actual managerial practice in local companies in comparable businesses.

The study is designed to be exploratory. Comparative management is inherently complex, and such theoretical models as do exist are too broad to provide meaningful hypotheses. In the present stage of development, a concentrated verification of a narrowly stated hypothesis would be premature. Instead, the pressing need now is for better knowledge upon which to construct insightful yet testable hypotheses. Consequently, this study casts a wide net in an effort to identify where, in fact, key differences do lie and which factors seem to be most influential.

However, since dealing with all the tasks of management — namely planning, organising, leading and controlling — would have been extremely difficult to reconcile with the kind of in-depth orientation desirable in an exploratory study, we chose to concentrate on control. There has been almost no comparative research on the control function, which is nevertheless felt to be of utmost interest for several reasons.

First, in the current era of scarce resources, control has become central to management to get efficient use of the resources it can muster.

Second, organisations have become more complex and diverse in their activities, larger in size and, as a result, require more decentralisation of decision-making and partial decomposition of objectives into separate units. Still, any organisation has to continue to harness all its efforts towards the accomplishment of common goals; it is the responsibility of top management to keep all organisation members, decisions and actions going in the same direction. In this environmental and structural context, the control function has not only become more important, it has also acquired an enlarged significance. It is no longer only a question of keeping track *ex post* of performance and then trying to explain and set corrective action; such hindsight, common in budgetary control, is often too late. Instead, management control is coming to mean the ability of an individual manager — and particularly a top manager — to note what is currently happening or, better, what is likely to happen in his organisation, and to take appropriate steps before the process is completed.

Finally, among the four management tasks, it seems that the implementation of control is the one which can lead to the greatest number of problems. If the final objective of control is to induce corrective action in any particular field of decision-making, several intermediate steps must be taken. Objectives have to be translated into operational standards, then performance has to be measured and the results communicated through

Introduction

the proper information system and, finally, observed performance has to be compared to projected standards. In each of these three steps, one tries to ensure that individuals or groups comply with set objectives (whether set unilaterally or by negotiation). Thus, control is perhaps the most 'behaviourally loaded' component of management – the one that depends most on the responses of people. Consequently, one can expect that cultural factors will play an even larger role in control than in other functions of management.

SCOPE OF THE STUDY

This research investigates, first, the similarities and differences in management control practices across countries and, second, what kinds of factors appear to account for the observed differences.

Broadly stated, the phenomena being studied is how the top managements of organisations in different countries make sure they get where they want to go.

This subject has been explored through an empirical investigation of comparable firms in three countries – France, Germany, Great Britain – which are each, according to previous research, representatives of a different 'cultural cluster'. As there has been little comparative research on actual management processes, an empirical orientation which is both comparative *and* in-depth in an exploratory way has been chosen as the best approach for getting a feel for the *reality* of practices. A fairly large sample of firms (52) was selected and a sizeable number of executives interviewed in the field (around 180). In the ten-month field-study, the researcher collected information by means of intensive personal interviews, and also from company control documents. In each country, questions were asked covering formal aspects of control, such as the following:

What are the objectives pursued in control?

How much time, effort and which emphases are given to control at the top management level?

How does the chief executive personally monitor performance?

What formal systems, procedures, rules and techniques have been set up to define objectives, measure performance and evaluate it?

How effective are they?

How are these systems used at operational levels in marketing and production?

With what results?

An analysis of *comparative* management control processes does not imply as was often the case in previous research, that universal concepts and principles will not also prevail. While it may be true that certain national characteristics may influence management control, these are not necessarily the only important influences. In order to sharpen our understanding of managing across countries, this research has deliberately included not only country factors but also the mainstream of thought on modern management theory. Thus, the technology and market within which the firms operated, their structural patterns of organisation, their main objectives, the planning activities they carried out and their management styles were also taken into account. Throughout, the interest was to see to what extent these factors as well as country forces may influence or explain control practices. The outcome of this exploratory investigation is a set of propositions on the relative impact of country variables and of such universal influences on management as technology and market structure. These propositions should help to bridge the gap between the universalist school and the culture-bound comparative school of management theory.

ORGANISATION OF THE BOOK

Part One sets the stage and defines the issues. The first chapter covers the current state of the art so as to set priorities for this research in the context of what previous research has already accomplished. The second chapter delineates more precisely what is meant by control in this study, and its dimensions are discussed. The independent contextual variables which may have an impact on control are also examined. In Chapter 3, the research design, methodology and tools are presented in full detail.

Part Two gives pride of place to the primary objective of the study, which is to delineate cross-national differences and similarities in control practices. Descriptive in nature, this part starts in Chapter 4 by presenting the contextual structural framework within which firms operate in each country and then examines their planning activities. Chapter 5 focuses on the chief executive's mode of control in the different countries: what does he use control for, what emphasis does he give to it, what does he control, when and how? Chapter 6 focuses on the 'controllership' function across countries in order to apprehend the design and use of formal systems which have been set up in each country, especially in the financial area. Chapter 7 finishes Part Two by looking at the use of control by line managers in two areas: marketing and production.

Part Three is interpretative. Having assessed cross-country differences and similarities, the report turns to the second priority of the research – i.e., explanation. Thus, Chapter 8 addresses the relative impact of country variables.

Finally, in Chapter 9 the findings with respect to country differences and the apparent reasons for them are related to various management theories. Some theories are supported, others challenged. The research concludes with a set of propositions suggesting orientations for further research in this area of comparative management and some hints for management improvement.

Part One
Setting the Stage

1 Comparative Management: The Current State of the Art

SCOPE OF CHAPTER

After the objectives and scope of comparative management are defined, a classification and analysis of past research in this area reveals that no study on control as a management process has been done so far. It has either been treated superficially as part of larger studies on management practices in general or only parts of control have been studied.[1] Most frequently, control has been studied from the point of view of the multinational corporation[2] and thus not truly cross-nationally. The analysis also reveals that findings are too inconclusive and contradictory to permit identification of solidly based *a priori* hypotheses. In fact, all authors concur on the need for more empirical, operational research before we can usefully set down some hypotheses. The general issue is whether or not management principles are universal and hence transferable. The means of pursuing the question chosen here is to see whether or not data on control practices from three European nations can best be explained by referring to universalist management principles or to some of the more differentiated models drawn from work in comparative management.

Given the relatively undeveloped status of work in the area of control practices, this study will necessarily be largely exploratory in nature, and will draw as much on comparative management theory for its theoretical orientations.

COMPARATIVE MANAGEMENT: OBJECTIVES AND SCOPE OF THE FIELD

Comparative management has been burgeoning in the 1960s with theories, conceptual models and field research conducted from the US and, as such, is not a very old field. Most scholars refer to Harbison and Myers[3] as one of the first attempts to see what is outside American management. The field grew out of concern about the universality of management concepts, theories and methodologies. Multinational corporations were developing around the world and some questions arose as to whether one should manage foreign and domestic operations in a similar way. Early mistakes, or even blunders, made by managers when abroad warned them that something might be different there.

Many people, although not all, regard the problem of comparative management as one of transferring American management knowledge and practice to less developed countries. A more useful approach consists in asking whether or not existing management theory, concepts and practices can be applied everywhere and then, if there are differences, to evaluate to what extent they will be affected by the external environment (political, economic, social and cultural forces prevailing in a country) and finally to assess what will work best in a given situation.

There are many definitions of the field of comparative management. Boddewyn[4] defines it as 'Dealing with cross-cultural similarities and differences among actors, processes, structures, functions and environmental interactions.'

That is, comparing managers as to who they are (actors); what they do (process); how they are related to other people (structures); what they contribute (function in society) and how they interact with their milieu (interaction with environment).

A second definition is the one given by H. Schöllhammer:

Comparative management theory can ... be defined as being concerned with the systematic detection, identification, explanation and evaluation of uniformities and differences of managerial phenomena in different countries or regions. The analysis of the management-relevant similarities and variations in a comparative fashion forms then a basis for predictive statements about the degree of managerial effectiveness and productive efficiency and the improvement thereof.[5]

The common concerns in these and many other definitions are that comparative management involves the study of similarities and differences in management in different countries, the derivation of explanations for these differences and similarities and the determination of what works best in a particular region or country.

The field being young, there is no further consensus or refinement at this point in terms of comparison (what to compare: actors, processes, function?), in terms of explanation (what variables are likely to explain most of the differences?), in terms of the measurement of effectiveness (how to measure system, or firm, or subsystem effectiveness?), or in terms of which countries or regions to compare (what specific countries are most interesting to compare?).

CRITICAL ISSUES IN COMPARATIVE MANAGEMENT

The field is young and this youth accounts for the highly dispersed and unsystematic character of the findings (see Neghandi[6]) and in attempted syntheses such as the ones provided by Boddewyn,[7] Roberts,[8] Nath,[9] Barrett and Bass[10] and Schöllhammer.[11]

Opinions concur to link effective management with economic progress[12,13] as shown in figure 1.1.[14]

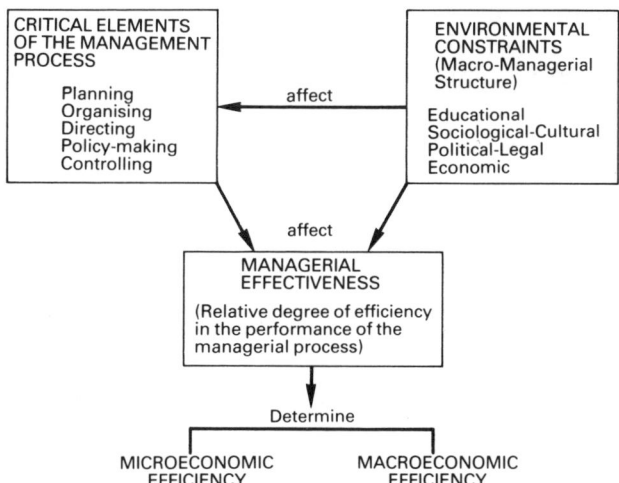

FIG. 1.1 The Farmer–Richman model

However there has not yet been clear evidence that management is universal. Until such evidence exists, *a priori* hypothesis must be that it is not and researchers may expect to find differences in management from country to country.

The critical questions to be asked and answered in comparative studies are the following:

What practices prevail in different countries?

How do these practices differ from one country to the other?

What accounts for these differences? Is it cultural, educational, political, sociological or economic factors?

How effective are the prevailing practices?

Reliable knowledge about differences in management practices between countries has several potential uses:

Local managers can learn from each other. What works well elsewhere and what accounts for different emphasis can give clues for local improvements.

Multinational managers can be much more adept in designing their management system abroad to fit local philosophies if differing too much from headquarters practice.

Management theory can be made more realistic by disproving some hypotheses (such as the universal nature of management principles) or supporting others.

In view of past research and findings three key issues can now be identified and these give priorities for comparative management studies.

THE UNIVERSALITY ISSUE

Paramount among these issues is the controversial problem of the applicability of universal principles across countries. in this respect three tendencies have emerged:

(a) One tendency – represented by Koontz,[15] Harbison and Myers[16] and Fayerweather[17] – holds that management is exportable, is indissolubly linked to economic progress and industrialisation and that – even if practices may differ – the theory, in its fundamentals, is the same all over.

In this view, thus, standardisation of multinational corporations management design is the key to success. Local management can learn effectively from the most effective and advanced practices wherever they are located. Management theory does not need any 'cultural' contingencies.

Up to now, however, evidence of such universality is not conclusive.

(b) A second school of thought claims just the opposite. Each country has its own legal, political, cultural and economic environment which will influence managerial behaviour and effectiveness and one must be careful when viewing management abroad or managing abroad. Representatives of this tendency are: Webber,[18] Robock,[19] Farmer and Richman,[20] Negandhi,[21] Oberg[22] and Gonzales and McMillan Jr.[23]

In this view, multinational managers must be constantly aware of constraining forces in each country in which they operate and refrain from standardisation. In fact they must fit management design to local conditions prevailing in each country.

Local management must refrain from learning from foreign practices. They must rather look for the most effective practices in their own country for guidance. Management theory is culture-bound and generalisation is dangerous.

This 'nationalistic' view is in fact disproved by many successes of companies abroad, such as IBM in Japan. It is much less in order in view of the cross-fertilisation process which has occurred together with the degree of economic interdependence between countries.

(c) A third approach is middle of the road as it tries to cluster countries together,[24,25] looking for group similarities like the Nordic-European, the Latin-European and so forth. To date, the results have not been entirely clear-cut. For instance, in the Haire *et al.* study of managerial attitudes, only 30 per cent of the variance could be explained by national differences. In the Sehti study, nations clustered differently depending on what factor was included in the analysis.

Clustering countries into groups with similar patterns is of course of prime interest both to local managers and multinational managers.

So far, however, the universality issue is not solved. Comparing countries on particular dimensions and, if differences are seen, to infer that they are culturally determined is too narrow a view to be useful. This type of study has been labelled the 'black box approach' to comparative management.[26]

What are the determinants of culture? Which variables affect which managerial behaviour? These questions have not received operational answers yet. Models have been suggested by Farmer and Richman,[27] Negandhi[28] and Estafen[29] which list environmental country variables (such as educational, economic, sociological, political and legal factors) to account for culture. They are useful in alerting us that culture does not only encompass norms of society but also environmental factors, but which factor leads to which behaviour has yet to be proved.[30]

So far, therefore, there is no consistent proof that management is culture-bound or not, nor are there tight conceptual models in terms of which to study the influence of country factors on management processes.

As Negandhi puts it:

In comparative management studies, there is an implicit assumption that not only are attitudes a function of culture, but that particular managerial attitudes lead to specific behavior and that this behavior is linked to management effectiveness. This may very well be the case but *empirical evidence is lacking* to support it.[31]

As a result we must be more modest in only considering that country forces may influence management processes such as control.

In fact, as sufficient mastery of the field is not yet available, culture cannot be defined very precisely. As a result, the research refers preferably to a *cross-national study* of management control practices rather than *cross-cultural* or any other more precise concepts on which it would not be possible to elaborate in the design. This view has been taken by a number of authors. For instance, Nath states: 'We mean by cross-cultural research,

Comparative Management: The State of the Art

research undertaken for comparative puposes across several different national populations or equivalent sections'.[32]

In this view, our aim must be to add empirical evidence to help locating influences on management practices. This view has been voiced by many authors like Barrett and Bass who have asked for 'a moratorium' on conceptual models[33] and argue that 'the greatest need is for more empirical research which will allow us to put more pieces in the puzzle'.[34]

THE MISSING LINK BETWEEN COMPARATIVE MANAGEMENT AND EXISTING MANAGEMENT THEORIES

Especially for the non-universalist schools of comparative management, there have been few links between comparative management and management theories and concepts. For example, work developed in Anglo-Saxon countries on organisational structure has not been utilised:

> Another notable lack in all these studies is the identification of the managers' organisation. Relatively sophisticated techniques and frameworks have evolved for classifying organisations (Harvey, Perrow, Woodward, Lawrence and Lorsch). Yet none of these frameworks have been used in comparative management studies and this considerably limits on future generalisations.[35]

This is quite understandable as comparative management scholars have focused their conceptualisation on environmental (i.e., country) forces. However, in doing so they have deprived themselves of well-defined management concepts, even if these are often too normative and too 'Americanised'.

Depriving comparative management studies and findings from the body of knowledge of management theory can only reinforce 'cultural explanations'. In order to gain a better understanding of why certain characteristics differ, the researcher must be alert both to the potential explanation by country forces and the potential explanation from management theory and concepts.

The practitioner will gain in perspective. If some behaviour witnessed is 'country-bound' little can be learned and used from other countries without changing the basic country forces restraining change. If, however, explanation is 'country-free' a lot can be learned and used from others.

As a result, one of the tasks of this research is to bring one of the mainstreams of thought in management theory into the study design and to try to use it alongside a careful examination of environmental 'cultural' data, to explain how control practices work in these countries.

THE NEED FOR PROCESS-ORIENTED STUDIES

Related to the need for integration of management theory with cross-country findings, scholars in the field have focused their analysis much more on who the manager is, what he believes and how he interacts with his milieu than on what he does (processes) except in general terms, describing a process for an entire nation (e.g. the empirical work done in Chile, Spain, Uruguay, the Philippines, Turkey, Denmark, India, Argentina, Brazil, Spain[36]), or even several nations at once (e.g. the work of Granick in Europe,[37] Davis and Lauterbach in Latin America,[38] B. Gussman in Africa[39]).

In fact, most process-oriented studies — and for that matter most control studies — have been done in the international business field.

Models exist in the international business field and focus on how to operate abroad from the operator's point of view (a mixed strategy between local and home-made management). They are represented by Perlmutter,[40] Robock and Simmonds,[41] Vernon,[42] Zenoff and Zwick,[43] Rutenberg[44] and Blough.[45]

Empirically this has led to studying the view of the countries of origin for a single or several multinational corporations and their resulting behaviour towards their subsidiaries (how they structure their operations abroad, how they control them, how they communicate with their subsidiaries, how they formulate standard marketing or financial policies, how they plan for world-wide operations, etc.). In this respect, examples run from multinational behaviour abroad[46] to specific behaviour in a particular country — as Brandt and Hulbert in Brazil[47] — to in-house studies of research in one multinational corporation.[48] However, this orientation, interesting from the multinational corporation's point of view, may distract the analysis from local management practices, as the multinational may impose its home-country point of view.

Focusing on multinational corporations to draw conclusions about the relative importance or lack of importance of universal or 'country' forces is not central to the purpose of comparative management. Multinational corporations by their mere size and sophistication may not give an 'average' representation of management practices. Besides if no comparisons are made (as often is the case) between their behaviour in a foreign country and local practices — and of the relative effectiveness of each — it is difficult to sort out the impact of local factors and home-country factors.

As a consequence of past foci—either too general or too narrow or oriented solely towards multinationals—we do not yet have conceptual models specifically focusing on control across countries on which further research can build.

IMPLICATIONS FOR THIS RESEARCH

After ten to fifteen years of research in comparative management it has been recognised that past research has had the merit of exploring a new field, creating new orientations and new ideas:

> Comparative management studies have had the salutary effects of making us look at other philosophies and practices and forcing us to question the unqualified universality of our management principles.[49]

However, critiques in the field have become stronger as to the concepts, designs, methodologies and content usefulness of existing research. In fact, most authors conclude at this point that:

1. New research should be empirical and not conceptual[50]
2. A 'marriage is needed' between management theory and comparative management[51]
3. The focus of research should be on processes more than on the individual manager's attitudes or background[52]
4. Finally, more research is needed which is of practical value,

away from descriptions of elites and macro-economic models,[5,3] asking some hard-nosed operational questions.

These priorities have been selected as the basis of the research presented.

In addition, as management processes across countries have been seen in general, authors have suggested that such lack of focus has prevented inferring useful propositions and concepts for comparative study. By focusing in depth on one process—control—and not all processes, we hope to better derive such propositions.

However, as no previous study of management processes has been so structured, this one will necessarily be exploratory in nature and thus we must first look at whether differences prevail across countries; in what way they prevail and explanations both from the universalist school (i.e., current management theory) and the non-universalist school (i.e., country forces).

SUMMARY

In this chapter, the *objectives* and *scope* of the comparative management field have been defined. Examination of a number of empirical studies has led to the conclusion that research styles and findings thus far tend to be widely divergent, and sometimes unrelated. It seems likely that attempts to construct overall systemic explanations have been premature. As a result, the need is for more focused research (e.g., to study not all management practices but parts of such practices like control), more oriented towards processes ('how to' types of questions). Analysis of the findings available in the field suggest that the best strategy for this research is an exploratory in-depth cross-national study of management control practices. Current criticisms of the field have led to the definition of priorities for conducting this research which are:

1. to be empirical in nature
2. to be oriented more towards actual practice than conceptualisation
3. to be oriented towards processes
4. to be focused on one area of management processes

Comparative Management: The State of the Art 19

5. to pay close attention both to the management theory approach to control and the influence of country factors.

The next chapter defines the focus of attention (control) and introduces the main management theory concepts as well as possible country factors to keep in view while studying control practices.

NOTES

1. R. N. Farmer and B. M. Richman, 'A Model for Research in Comparative Management', *California Management Review*, vol. 2, no. 2 (Winter 1964) and *International Business: an Operational Theory* (Homewood, Ill.: Richard D. Irwin, 1966); see also A. R. Negandhi and B. D. Estafen, 'A Research Model to Determine the Applicability of American Know-How in Different Cultures and/or Environments', *Academy of Management Journal*, vol. 8, no. 4 (December 1965) pp. 319–28; and M. Haire, E. E. Ghiselli, L. W. Porter, *Managerial Thinking: an International Study* (New York: John Wiley & Sons, 1966) ch. 2.
2. M. Z. Brooke and H. L. Rammers, *The Strategy of Multinational Enterprise* (London: Longman Group Ltd., 1970) ch. 4; S. H. Robock and K. Simmonds, *International Business and Multinational Enterprises* (Homewood, Ill.: R. D. Irwin, 1973) ch. 18; J. Stopford and L. T. Wells, *Managing the Multinational Enterprise* (New York: Basic Books, 1972); D. P. Rutenberg, 'Organizational Archetypes of a Multinational Company', *Management Science*, vol. 16, no. 6 (February 1970) pp. B337–B349; D. B. Zenoff and J. Zwick, *International Financial Management* (Englewoods Cliffs, N.J.: Prentice Hall, 1969); W. K. Brandt, J. M. Hulbert, 'Patterns of Communications in the Multinational Corporation's: an Empirical Study', Research Paper, no. 76 (New York: Columbia University, Graduate School of Business, 1974).
3. F. H. Harbison and C. A. Myers, *Management in the Industrial World* (New York: McGraw Hill, 1959).
4. J. Boddewyn, *Comparative Management and Marketing* (Scott, Foresman and Co., 1969) p. 43.
5. H. Schöllhammer, 'Strategies in Comparative Management Theorizing', in J. Boddewyn (ed.), *Comparative Management Proceedings* (New York: New York University, Graduate School of Business, 1970) p. 14.
6. A. R. Negandhi, 'Cross-Cultural Management Studies: too many Conclusions not enough Conceptualization', *Management International Review* (1974).
7. J. Boddewyn (ed.), *Comparative Management, Teaching, Training, Research* (New York: New York University Press, 1970) ch. 8, p. 208.
8. K. H. Roberts and W. K. Graham (ed.), *Comparative Studies in*

Organizational Behaviour (New York: Holt, Rinehart and Winston, 1972).
9. R. Nath, 'A Methodological Review of Cross Cultural Management Research', *International Social Science Journal* (Spring 1968).
10. G. V. Barrett and B. R. Bass, 'Comparative Surveys of Managerial Attitudes and Behaviour', in J. Boddewyn (ed.) *Comparative Management Teaching, Training, Research.*
11. H. Schöllhammer, 'Strategies and Methodologies in International Business and Comparative Management', *Management International Review* (1973/6).
12. R. N. Farmer and B. M. Richman, *Comparative Management and Economic Progress* (Homewood, Ill.: R. D. Irwin, 1965).
13. W. W. Rostow, *The Stages of Economic Growth* (Cambridge, Mass.: Harvard University Press, 1962), p. 17.
14. R. N. Farmer and B. M. Richman, 'A Model for Research in Comparative Management', *California Management Review*, vol. II, no. 2 (December 1964).
15. H. Koontz, 'A Model for Analysing the Universality and Transferability of Management', *Academy of Management Journal*, vol. 12, no. 4 (December 1969) pp. 415–29.
16. F. H. Harbison and C. A. Myers, op. cit., p. 117.
17. J. Fayerweather, *The Executive Overseas* (Syracuse University Press, 1959).
18. R. A. Webber, *Management* (Homewood Ill.: R. D. Irwin, 1975) ch. 11, pp. 228–42.
19. S. H. Robock and K. Simmonds, op. cit., ch. 11, pp. 239–69.
20. R. N. Farmer and B. M. Richman, 'A Model for Research in Comparative Management', *California Management Review*, vol. 7 (Winter 1964) pp. 55–68.
21. A. R. Negandhi, 'A Model for Analysing Organizations in Cross-Cultural Settings: a Conceptual Scheme and Some Research Findings', in Comparative Administration and Management Conference, *Bureau of Economic and Business Research* (Ohio: Kent State University, 1968) pp. 55–87.
22. W. Oberg, 'Cross-Cultural Perspectives on Management Principles', *Academy of Management Journal*, vol. 6, no. 2 (June 1963).
23. R. F. Gonzales and C. McMillan, 'The Universality of American Management Philosophy', *Academy of Management Journal*, vol. 4, no. 1 (1961), pp. 33–4.
24. S. P. Sehti and D. Curry, 'Variable and Object Clustering of Cross-Cultural Data: Some Implications for Comparative Research and Policy Formulation', in S. P. Sethi and J. N. Sheth, *Multinational Business Operations, Long-Range Planning, Organization and Management* (Calif.: Goodyear Publishing Co., 1973) pp. 14–49.
25. M. Haire *et al.*, op. cit.
26. M. Ajiferuke and J. Boddewyn, 'Culture and other Explanatory Variables in Comparative Management Studies', *Academy of Management Journal*, vol. 8, no. 2 (June 1970).

27. R. N. Farmer and B. M. Richman, *International Business: An Operational Theory* (Homewood, Ill.: R. D. Irwin, 1966).
28. A. R. Negandhi and B. D. Estafen, 'A Research Model to Determine the Applicability of American Know-How in Different Cultures and/or Environments', *Academy of Management Journal*, vol. 8, no. 4 (December 1965).
29. B. D. Estafen, 'Methods for Management Research in the 1970s: An Ecological System Approach', *Academy of Management Journal* (March 1971).
30. H. Schöllhammer, op. cit.
31. A. R. Negandhi, 'Cross-cultural Management Studies: too many Conclusions not enough Conceptualization', *Management International Review* (1974/6) pp. 61–7.
32. R. Nath, 'A Methodological Review of Cross-Cultural Management Research', in J. Boddewyn (ed.), *Comparative Management and Marketing*, p. 196.
33. G. V. Barrett and B. R. Bass, 'Comparative Surveys of Managerial Attitudes and Behavior', in J. Boddewyn (ed.), *Comparative Management, Teaching, Training, Research*.
34. Ibid., p. 209.
35. Ibid., ch. 8, p. 206.
36. B. D. Estafen, 'An Empirical Experiment in Comparative Management: A Study of the Transferability of American Management Policies and Practices into Firms Operating in Chile', op. cit.; A. R. Negandhi, 'American Management Abroad: A Comparative Study of Management Practices of American Subsidiaries and Local Firms in Developing Countries', op. cit.; A. R. Negandhi and S. B. Prasad, *Comparative Management* (New York: Appleton-Century-Crofts, 1970). M. E. Douglass, 'Testing a Methodology for Measuring the Interaction, between Organization and Environment', *Management International Review*, vol. 15, no 1 (1975) pp. 89–97, tested the systems transfer characteristics model of B. D. Estafen. No significant differences were seen between groups of Danish firms and US subsidiaries. G. P. Lauter, 'Environmental Constraints Impeding Managerial Performance in Developing Countries', *Management International Review*, vol. 10, nos. 2–3 (1970) pp. 45–52, testing the Farmer–Richman model in eight Turkish and US subsidiaries, found no significant differences. B. D. Estafen, 'Methods for Management Research in the 1970s: an Ecological Systems Approach', *Academy of Management Journal* (March 1971) pp. 51–64 and also B. D. Estafen, 'The Systems Transfer Characteristics of Firms in Spain: a Comparative Management Study' (Indiana University: Graduate School of Business, International Research Series, Number 5).
37. D. Granick, *The European Executive* (New York: Doubleday and Co, 1962).
38. A. Lauterbach, *Enterprise in Latin America* (Ithaca: Cornell University Press, 1966); S. Davis, 'US vs Latin America Business and Culture', *Harvard Business Review* (November 1969).

39. B. Gussman, *Out in the Midday Sun* (New York: Oxford University Press 1963) comparison of Africans with Europeans.
40. H. U. Perlmutter, 'L'Entreprise Internationale. Trois Conceptions', *Revue Economique et Sociale*, vol. 23, no. 2 (May, 1965); developing ethnocentric, polycentric and geocentric management philosophies leading to regulatory, permissive or cooperative styles of behaviour.
41. S. H. Robock and K. Simmonds, op. cit.
42. R. Vernon, *Sovereignty at Bay: the Multinational Spread of US Entreprises* (New York: Basic Books, 1971).
43. D. B. Zenoff and J. Zwick, op. cit.
44. D. P. Rutenberg, op. cit.
45. R. Blough, *International Business: Environment and Adaptation* (New York: McGraw Hill, 1966).
46. M. Z. Brooke and H. L. Rammers, op. cit.; R. J. Alsegg, 'Control Relationships between American Corporations and their European Subsidiaries', *American Management Association*, Research Study no. 107 (1971).
47. For instance, W. K. Brandt and J. M. Hulbert, 'Marketing Strategies of American, European and Japanese Multinational Subsidiaries', paper presented at the Academy of International Business Meetings (Fontainebleau, France: 7–9 July 1975).
48. D. Sirota and J. M. Greenwood, 'Understand Your Overseas Work Force', *Harvard Business Review*, vol. 49, no. 1 (1971) pp. 53–60; D. Sirota, 'International Survey of Job Goals and Beliefs', paper presented at the 16th International Congress of Applied Psychology (Amsterdam, 1968); see also for a discussion: A. I. Krantz, IBM, 'Some Recent Advances in Cross-National Management Research', *Academy of Management Journal*, vol. 18, no. 3 (1975) pp. 538–49; Pjotr Hesserling, 'Studies in Cross-Cultural Organization', *Columbia Journal of World Business* (December 1973); Philipps and J. W. Slocum Jr, 'A Comparative Study of American and Mexican Operatives', *Academy of Management Journal*, vol. 14, no. 1 (March 1971) pp. 89–97 (used Porter need-satisfaction questionnaire in a glass company).
49. M. Ajiferuke and J. Boddewyn, op. cit., p. 161.
50. G. V. Barrett and B. M. Bass, op. cit., p. 209.
51. A. R. Negandhi, 'Comparative Management and Organization Theory: A Marriage Needed', *Academy of Management Journal*, vol. 18, no. 2 (June 1975) p. 340; G. F. Farris and D. A. Butterfield, 'Control Theory in Brazilian Organizations', *Administrative Science Quarterly*, vol. 17 (1972) pp. 574–85; J. T. McMahon, J. M. Ivancevich, 'A Study of Control in a Manufacturing Organization, Managers and Non-Managers', *Administrative Science Quarterly*, vol. 21 (March 1976), when finding that technology was a determinant ingredient to control.
52. J. Boddewyn, *Comparative Management and Marketing* (Scott, Foresman and Co, 1969), p. 43.
53. K. H. Roberts, 'On Looking at an Elephant: an Evaluation of Cross-Cultural Research Related to Organizations', *Psychological Bulletin* (November 1970).

2 Management Control and Associated Variables

SCOPE OF CHAPTER

This chapter sets forth the variables examined in the present study. First, the meaning and components of management control are described. Then a set of independent variables which may strongly influence control practice in specific companies are discussed. Besides country factors, which are commonly in use in comparative research, management theory suggests that attention be paid to the environment of the firm (technology and market), the strategy of the firm and other management processes (structure and planning). Each of these variables is subdivided to facilitate a detailed in-depth analysis of the control structure.

STRATEGY OF RESEARCH

Owing to the need for more focused empirical research, not knowing which specific country factors might influence which control processes and aware of the need to examine the applicability of mainstream management theory in this area, this research has chosen the following strategy:

(a) define the central topic (management control) in all its detailed facets and angles;
(b) look at country differences and similarities on these facets to see emerging patterns;
(c) include current management concepts for possible complementary analysis together with country factors.

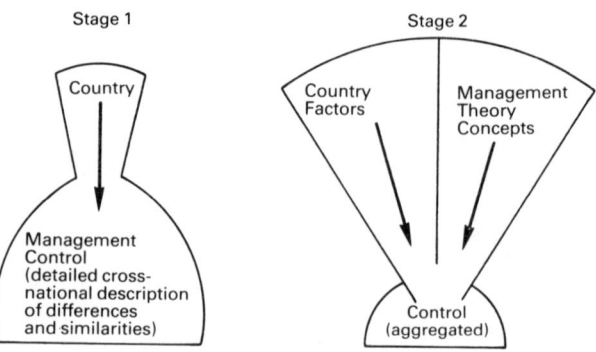

FIG. 2.1 Chosen strategy of research

The current state of the art is of little help in suggesting explicit *a priori* hypotheses about which country and/or which management variable will affect control in various ways. We prefer to: (a) be aware of possible concurrent influences; and (b) derive our propositions after the data are collected.

Our working hypothesis is thus a generally sceptical one – the evidence necessary to treat the problem is not in yet, and as we analyse our data we must be open to explanations both in terms of mainstream managerial principles and of individual country factors.

In order to do so, however, the data on management control will first be described from the perspective of differences and similarities between countries.

Next, they will be aggregated and analysis and tentative explanation will be attempted both in terms of plausible country factors and of selected management theory variables, as depicted in figure 2.1.

Let us now turn to the definition of control and associated variables (country and management concepts).

CONTROL AND CONTROLS

1. Control has different meanings in the business literature, depending on whether it is seen from the view point of the organisation looking towards the environment,[1] the organisation

towards the inside components (the management system), a group towards another group or an individual towards another individual.[2] A preliminary task of the researcher clearly is to state his area of interest, precisely delineating the research boundaries.

The study deals with management control which is a part of the job of the manager or of management together with organising, planning and leading and is defined as 'the process by which one ensures that performance is as near as practical to plan'.[3]

The full four-step control process can be depicted as in figure 2.2.[4]

This cybernetic view of control is the one mostly used in management literature when focusing on formal systems as opposed to the behavioural point of view which refers more to the amount of power (whether formal or informal) an individual or a group has over another individual or group.[5]

The first view is taken here in order to focus on internal management *processes* much more than on individual or group informal means of influencing other people. However, proponents of the former view are aware that control has to be accepted positively by the individuals if it is to be effective and thus the

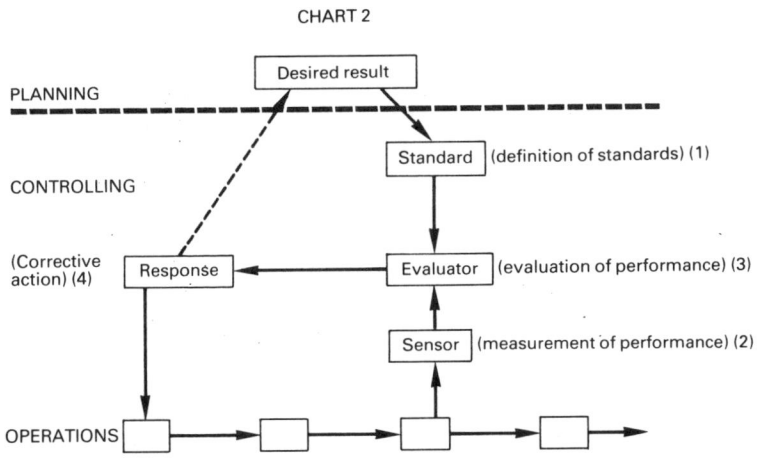

FIG. 2.2 The control process

responses of people will be taken into account. In this perspective management control is every manager's job.

Thus, the research could focus on the control activity of anybody who has some kind of responsibility in the firm. Such research, if empirical, could hardly investigate more than one or two organisations, which would defeat one of the objectives of the study, which is to compare. This is the reason why the current research deals only with control at the *top managerial* level.

As a result of the previous comments, the research scope can be more precisely defined as the empirical investigation of how top management tries to assure that performance is as near as practical to plan, in different local companies, in different countries.

Given the above definition of control, it is clear that control processes stand in some close relation to planning. It is beyond the scope of this research to get into a detailed description of planning; for our purposes it is enough to note that Steiner[6] has developed a useful analysis of the dimensions of planning and plans which is illustrated in figure 2.3.

As implied by Steiner in his close analysis of top management planning, control also has five key dimensions. Each of these dimensions can be studied in terms of key characteristics as shown in figure 2.4.

This figure, which serves to indicate the multi-dimensional complexity of the dependent variable, requires a number of comments.

First, as suggested by Steiner's treatment of planning, the key axes in this diagram of the control process each have a number of subdimensions or spheres or levels in terms of which control

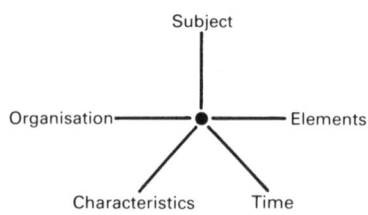

FIG. 2.3 Five key dimensions to planning

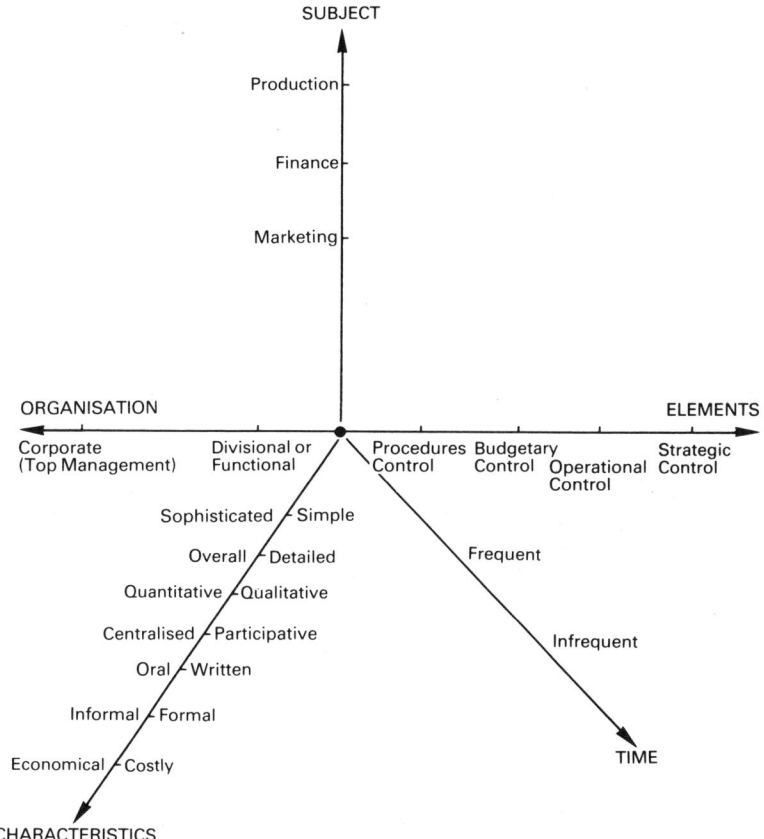

FIG. 2.4 Dimensions of control focused on subject

may be studied. Since the study is exploratory in nature, and as the design calls for research in three countries in which control practices were thought to be fairly different, it made sense to cast as wide a net as possible to include as many sub-dimensions and levels in the study as seemed relevant. This degree of detail permitted picking up certain country-specific patterns and attitudes, revealing, among other things, that the notion of control was interpreted in widely varying fashion.[7]

To reduce the magnitude of data collection, however, not all permutations among all features have been investigated. For example, strategic control is investigated only at the top two levels; formalism is a significant issue at operational levels.

Eventually to deal with the wide array of dimensions and features when relating them as dependent variables to independent variables, aggregated indexes have been built which permit associating control with the independent variables.

Finally, the following remarks will help to clarify the scope and meaning of the various dimensions identified.

Subject

Only three of the many areas of control are investigated: *production, marketing* and *financial* controls. These represent the main three functional areas of the firm. They are also less controversial in nature and easier to grasp than research and development or manpower for which planning is known to be more difficult.

Organisation

The main interest here is in knowing the level or location of control activity for each of the separate functions, the types of controls (see elements) used at various levels and how the control function itself is organised. Emphasis is given to the top management's role and to the formal control systems at work.

Characteristics

Informal—formal
Business history is full of examples in which top management had a good grasp of their business without formal systems of control. It is also full of examples of companies which had a major setback once the 'owner—entrepreneur—chief executive' retired, creating a void where nobody knew exactly what was going on (see for instance the Convair case where the company lost $500 million in three years because of lack of control after the retirement of Jay Hopkins).[8] The degree of formalism indicates the institutionalisation and durability of control.

Participative—centralised
Control activity can be performed largely by staff or it can be

widely delegated to those affected. The location of responsibility is closely related to the management style of a company.

Qualitative—quantitative
The degree of quantification in control highlights how top management and key functional executives are able to transform objectives into measurable standards against which to measure performance.

Overall—detailed
The degree of detail in control by top management affects not only information flows but also initiative and flexibility at operating levels.

Costly or economical
Control is but one of the many tasks of management. As noted by Ackoff, too often the computer has helped develop information systems which serve little purpose.[9] A significant aspect of every control system is how much it costs.

Time span
Controls can be frequent or infrequent. If too frequent, control does not facilitate any corrective action and the subordinates do not feel they have been given full responsibility. If not frequent enough, control may come too late to do anything and one is forced to downgrade plans. This research will investigate the frequency with which control is exercised for different subjects, elements and organisational levels. Planning and control horizons are also noted.

Elements

The linkage between planning and controlling is revealed by the subjects addressed in the control processes. Upon what is control focused? Possibilities include strategic goals, financial budgets, methods and procedures, delivery schedules, quality standards and employee morale. Clearly there can be no control of such matters unless plans are first formulated. On the other hand, the existence of plans (strategic, operational, actions programmes, budgets . . .) is no guarantee that control will follow. Consequently, a study of control 'elements' calls for considerable probing both about what kind of planning prevails and about just what is actually controlled.

Having outlined the meaning of control as used in this research and the different dimensions to be investigated, the research domain can now be summarised.

1. How, in different countries, does top management ensure that performance is as near as practical to plan in the areas of general management, marketing, production and finance?
2. In so doing, what processes are used; what characteristics do they have (formalism, degree of detail, cost, reporting); how frequently are they used; how are they organised?
3. Finally, on what elements do these controls bear (strategy, operational plans, action programmes, budgets and procedures)?

INDEPENDENT VARIABLES INVESTIGATED

It is unreasonable to assume that country variables will be the only influences on differences in managerial control. In specific companies, a variety of additional independent variables will probably affect the control system in use. We shall try in this study to minimise the effect of technology and company size by careful selection of the companies studied in each country. But to really understand why an observed control pattern exists, we should observe several other factors likely to have an impact in conjunction with country differences.

Management theory suggests two types of independent variables to be investigated: 'business' variables (i.e., technology, market stability and strategy) and 'management system' variables (i.e., structure and planning). Using this classification the basic research design then can be visualised as follows in figure 2.5.

BUSINESS VARIABLES

Business variables refer to the kinds of market and the technology a firm has chosen by defining its own strategy. In fact, when we look at the development of modern management theory, we can see it has followed a pendular movement.

Classical management theory, represented by Fayol,[10]

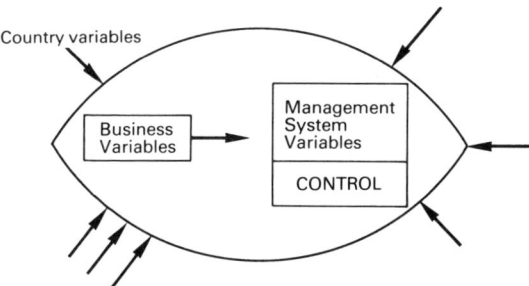

FIG. 2.5 Variables influencing control

Taylor[11] and Gulick,[12] focused on deliberately designed managerial arrangements such as division of labour, coordination, hierarchical responsibilities. This approach, which may be called Theory X, focused on a formal arrangement of work which is presumed to be optimally organised. This view has been succeeded by the human relations school, represented by Argyris,[13] Likert[14] and Herzberg,[15] — often called Theory Y — which focuses on the integration of the individual in the organisation and presents alternative ways of meeting the needs of individuals. In their view, an organisation was optimised by using motivating forces to fulfil the needs of the individuals which are in many cases opposed to the principles developed in Theory X.

Now, the latest trend in the development of management theory is that there is no one best way to manage but that '*it all depends*' (this is even the title of a book by Sherman[16] after his experience with the New York Port Authority). It means, for instance, that one cannot say each supervisor should always have a limited number of subordinates as the classical school might say; or that a democratic leadership style will always work, as sometimes inferred from Theory Y. This contingency theory tries to classify much more positively and systematically under which conditions or circumstances one type of management arrangements is likely to be better. As a result, recent books in management, instead of being of the check list type (do's and don'ts) are now more oriented towards two by two matrices as in figure 2.6.

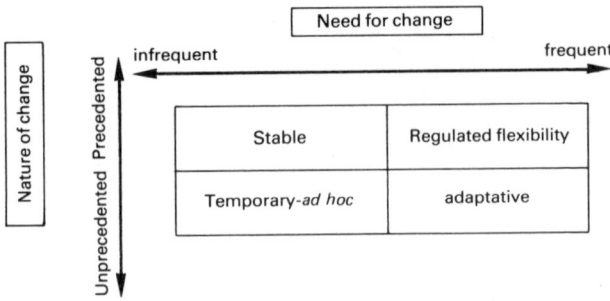

FIG. 2.6 Influence of technology and market change on the type of management design

As to the circumstances or conditions under which a particular type of management setting will work, three main classes have emerged. Some authors like Woodward,[17] Perrow,[18] and Dubin,[19] have focused more on the influence of *technology* on all management processes (organising, planning, leading, controlling) or on parts thereof. Some others, like Lawrence and Lorsch,[20] and Burns and Stalker,[21] insisted more on the influence of the *market* environment on management process or parts thereof. Newman[22] has developed a framework (see figure 2.6) which takes into account both influences.

Finally, some authors like Chandler,[23] Greiner,[24] Learned et al.[25] and Bruce Scott[26] have focused on the influence of *objectives* and *strategy* on management processes or parts thereof. For instance, a one-product company should be organised by functions, and a multi-product—multi-market firm by divisions or regions.

Following these trends, one should take into account technology, market environment and basic objectives and strategies to understand the management system of which control is a part. We will call these three variables '*business variables*' (see figure 2.7).

With respect to company strategy, the literature suggests attention be placed especially on diversification and growth objectives.

With respect to technology and market environment it suggests attention be placed on the degree of complexity[27] and rate of change.[28]

Management Control and Associated Variables

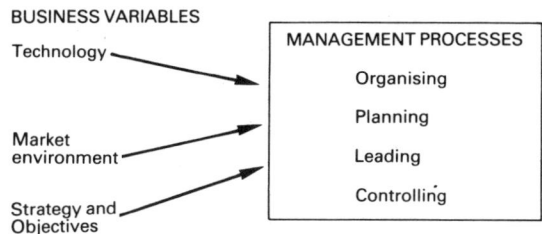

FIG. 2.7 Business variables

MANAGEMENT SYSTEM VARIABLES

The second group of independent variables relates to a company's internal management system to suit the particular strategy chosen within certain technologies and market segments. According to management theory presented in Newman *et al.*,[29] the different processes of organising, planning, leading and controlling are interrelated and effective management will stem not only from the balance between technology, market environment, strategy and the management processes but also from the internal coherence of the subprocesses themselves (see figure 2.8).

For instance, if a firm decentralises (process of organising) into profit centres, top management must measure performance (process of controlling) *overall* by a comprehensive device such as a monthly profit-and-loss statement. A lack of coherence in this respect will generate problems. Consequently, other subprocesses of management must be taken into account in the research on control.

According to Greiner,[30] at least one other business variable — namely size — affects the way a company will be organised and

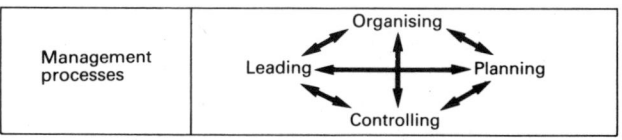

FIG. 2.8 Management system variables

led. The research design, defined in the next chapter, minimises the impact of size by keeping within comparable ranges.

With respect to organising, specific attention will be given to the division of labour, decentralisation in decision-making and to the instruments used for coordination. Under planning, we will consider who participates, the planning horizon, the content of recurring plans and a set of characteristics matching those applied to control (written plan leading to written control, etc.).

In the leading category, any link between rewards and punishments and control evaluation will be of specific interest, as well as the degree of employee participation in setting standards and interpreting results. However, because of the difficulty of obtaining data on leadership styles and motivation tools, leading activities will not be systematically investigated but mostly inferred from planning, organising and controlling activities.

COUNTRY VARIABLES

One of our primary emphases in this research is to look at country differences and similarities in a detailed fashion. Countries are compared with one another with respect to each of the many variables already discussed. This study does not undertake to categorise or analyse the attitudes, customs and values prevailing within a country. Nevertheless, a few 'cultural' variables have been so often linked to managerial practices in the literature that we should be sensitive to them in an exploratory study. They might throw considerable light on observed differences in control practices. Thus, they will be used concurrently with business and management system variables when tentative explanations are proposed.

Often mentioned in this regard is the *educational* background of top managers. An array of attitudes and values are often associated with technical training, prestige university experience, professional business education, etc., and some studies show that such associated values do affect management practice.[31]

Also, economic and social pressure arising from unemployment, inflation and social unrest is reported to affect manager's willingness to take risks or to embrace new managerial methods.[32-34]

Responses to controls are affected by 'cultural' traits such as employees' attitudes towards authority and discipline, towards bureaucracy and centralism and towards initiative and autonomy.[35,36] No attempt has been made to measure these supplementary country variables directly, but we should be alert to their plausible impact when we attempt to formulate tentative hypotheses.

SUMMARY

As outlined above, the main thrust of this study is a close, careful look at control practices and at possible explanations of observed differences in three countries. Being unprecedented in both design and coverage, the study is necessarily exploratory. And because it is exploratory, we have divided both the dependent and independent variables into several facets and angles to be alert to their possible importance.

The basic design treats managerial control practices as the dependent variable and relates them to three independent variables: country, business and management system. However, to tap the richness of an in-depth study, a series of sub-variables have been flagged for attention. The resulting model is shown in figure 2.9.

A first analysis on detailed control variables will be done by country, treating each as a unit. On aggregated control character-

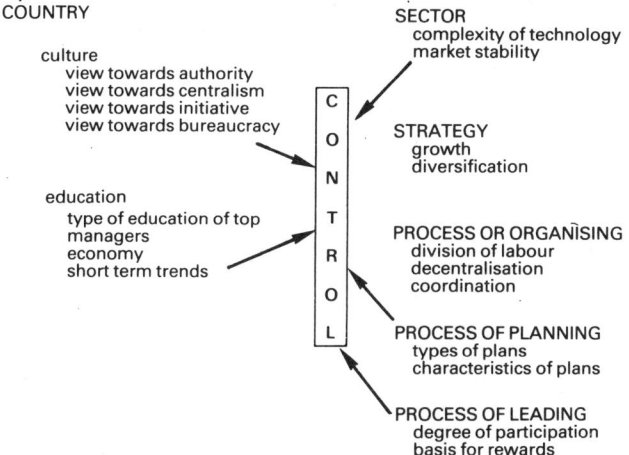

FIG. 2.9 A model for the study of control

istics, possible explanations will be presented through country variables, sector, strategy, organising, planning and leading processes.

The field study in which these variables were observed and recorded is described in the next chapter.

NOTES

1. As expressed in J. K. Galbraith, *The New Industrial State* (New York: Signet Books, 1968).
2. As depicted in G. W. Dalton and P. R. Lawrence, *Motivation and Control in Organizations* (Homewood, Ill.: R. D. Irwin and the Dorsey Press, 1971) p. 15.
3. W. H. Newman, *Constructive Control* (Englewood Cliffs, NJ: Prentice Hall, 1975).
4. Source after W. H. Newman: Constructive Control, op. cit.
5. A. S. Tannenbaum, 'Control in Organizations: Individual Adjustment and Organizational Performance', *Administrative Science Quarterly* vol. 2 (1962), pp. 236–57.
6. G. A. Steiner, *Top Management Planning* (New York: Macmillan Co., 1969) ch. 1.
7. As an indication, in France for instance, most executives interviewed started by saying that in the company control was not used in the American sense which was ' . . . '. In the process, the researcher obtained almost as many definitions of American control as the number of executives interviewed (around fifty).
8. 'The Convair Case', in W. H. Newman and J. P. Logan, *Strategy, Policy and Central Management* (South Western Publishing Co., 6th edn, 1971) p. 580.
9. R. L. Ackoff, *A Concept of Corporate Planning* (New York: John Wiley and Sons, 1970) ch. 6.
10. H. Fayol, *General and Industrial Management* (London: Pitman, 1949).
11. F. W. Taylor, *Principles of Scientific Management* (New York: Harper and Row, 1911).
12. L. Gulick and L. F. Urwick (ed.), *Papers on the Science of Administration* (New York: Columbia University, Institute of Public Administration, 1937).
13. C. Argyris, *Integrating the Individual and the Organization* (New York: John Wiley and Sons, 1964).
14. R. Likert, *New Patterns of Management* (New York: McGraw Hill Book Co., 1961).
15. F. Herzberg, B. Mausner and B. Snyderman, *The Motivation to Work* (New York: John Wiley and Sons, 1959).
16. Sherman, *It All Depends* (New York: American Management Association, 1970).

17. J. Woodward, *Industrial Organizations* (London: Oxford University Press, 1962).
18. C. Perrow, *Organizational Analysis: a Sociological View* (Belmont, Calif.: Wadsworth Publishing Co., 1970) ch. 3.
19. R. Dubin, 'Supervision and Productivity: Empirical Findings and Theoretical Considerations', in R. Dubin, G. Homans, F. Mann and D. Miller, *Leadership and Productivity* (Calif.: Chandler Publishing, 1965).
20. P. R. Lawrence and J. W. Lorsch, *Organization and Environment* (Cambridge, Mass.: Harvard Business School, Division of Research, 1967).
21. T. Burns and G. M. Stalker, *The Management of Innovation*, 2nd edn. (Tavistock Publications, 1962).
22. W. H. Newman, C. E. Summer, E. K. Warren, *The Process of Management*, 3rd edn. (Englewoods Cliffs, NH: Prentice Hall, 1972), p. 697.
23. A. D. Chandler, *Strategy and Structure* (Cambridge, Mass.: MIT Press, 1962).
24. L. A. Greiner, 'Evolutions and Revolutions as Organizations Grow', *Harvard Business Review* (July–August, 1972).
25. E. P. Learned, C. R. Christensen, K. R. Andrews and W. D. Guth, *Business Policy Text and Cases* (Homewood, Ill.: R. D. Irwin, 1969).
26. B. R. Scott, 'The Stages of Corporate Development', *Business Policy Notes 998,999* (Boston: Harvard University, Graduate School of Business Administration, 1971).
27. R. B. Duncan, 'Characteristics of Organization Environment', *Administrative Science Quarterly*, vol. 17, no. 3 (September 1972) pp. 313–27.
28. P. R. Lawrence and J. W. Lorsch, op. cit.
29. W. H. Newman, E. K. Warren, *The Process of Management*, 4th edn. (Englewood Cliffs, NJ: Prentice Hall, 1977), ch. 27.
30. L. A. Greiner, op. cit.
31. W. D. Guth and R. Tagiuri, 'Personal Values and Corporate Strategy', *Harvard Business Review* (May–June 1965) show the impact of personal values on decisions. Also, with respect to specific educational impact on management across countries, see D. Granick, *Managerial Comparisons of Four Developed Countries* (Cambridge, Mass.: MIT Press, 1972).
32. H. E. Wrapp, 'Good Managers Don't Make Policy Decisions', *Harvard Business Review* (September–October 1967) pp. 91–9
33. C. E. Lindblom, 'The Science of Muddling Through', *Public Administration Review*, vol. 19, no. 2 (Spring 1959).
34. R. M. Cyert and J. G. March, *A Behavioral Theory of the Firm* (Englewoods Cliffs, Prentice Hall, 1963).
35. Farmer and Richman provide a full list of such possible impacts: R. N. Farmer and B. M. Richman, *International Business, An Operational Theory* (Homewood, Ill.: R. D. Irwin, 1965).
36. See articles in Theodore D. Weinschall, *Culture and Management* (London, Penguin Books, 1977).

3 Research Design and Methodology

SCOPE OF CHAPTER

In this chapter, the criteria upon which the research design is based and the design itself are presented. For reasons discussed below, the latter includes local companies in three industrial sectors — electronics, textiles and engineering — in each of three countries: France, West Germany and Great Britain. Finally, the data collection process is described with emphasis on the selection of interviewees, the relationships between the variables selected in Chapter 2 (dependent and independent) and the measurement devices that have been used.

BASIC RESEARCH DESIGN

The criteria used in the research reflect the priorities set up in the review of comparative management research in Chapter 1, and the particular model of factors affecting managerial control developed in Chapter 2. More specifically:

1. to be able to compare several countries and companies must be dealt with.
2. to take into account modern management theory data on structure planning strategy have to be collected and technology and market stability controlled for.

The research design finally selected, after considering several different approaches, involved studying comparable sets of local companies in several different countries.

The criteria for selecting companies were:
(a) to draw from three diverse industry sectors, to assure an array of technological and market influences, but to use the *same sectors* in all countries — to obtain comparability between countries;
(b) to use only *local* companies — that is, not companies affiliated with a multinational organisation — to avoid 'contamination' of managerial systems imposed by foreign management;
(c) to select companies in the same size category — to avoid differences in control practices known to result from firm size.

To hold the entire project within the cost and time limitations of resources available, it was decided to select approximately five companies in each of three industrial sectors (following criteria described in the next section), for a total of fifteen companies per country. (Five companies per sector seem to be the minimum to allow for some kind of quantitative analysis.) Moreover, the countries chosen would necessarily be industrially advanced, large enough to offer a pool of firms of the types desired and near enough to each other geographically to meet cost and time considerations. For these reasons and for reasons having to do with the particular abilities of the author, European nations clearly seemed most suitable.

In choosing the countries, diversity of cultural characteristics was a primary goal, and for this purpose the classification developed by Haire *et al.*[2] was used.

The three countries selected were France, West Germany and Great Britain. As shown by Haire *et al.*, each country belongs to a different European cultural cluster. One is representative of the Latin-European culture, one is representative of the Anglo-

TABLE 3.1 Basic research design

	Great Britain	*Germany*	*France*	
Industry 1	5 local firms	5 local firms	5 local firms	= 15 firms
Industry 2	5 local firms	5 local firms	5 local firms	= 15 firms
Industry 3	5 local firms	5 local firms	5 local firms	= 15 firms
	15 firms	15 firms	15 firms	45 firms

Saxon culture and the other one is representative of the Nordic-European culture.

Thus, an initial presentation of the overall design would be as shown in Table 3.1.

CHOICE OF INDUSTRY SECTORS AND COMPANIES

CRITERIA FOR CHOOSING INDUSTRIES

As pointed out, technology and environment (market) affect management processes. The two following criteria have been used to select industries:

1. *Technological change and complexity*: defined as the degree of innovation in the process which transforms inputs into output and the degree of know-how and technical complexity needed
2. *Environment stability*: defined as the rate of change in market conditions (rapid changes in consumer behaviour, competitive moves, product substitution and innovation).

As a result, the industries have been selected as follows:

	Technological change and complexity	*Market change*
Industry 1	High	High
Industry 2	Medium	Medium
Industry 3	Low	Low

PRACTICAL CHOICE OF INDUSTRIES

A list of industries was drawn up and a classification in three categories was made according to the two criteria. This classification resulted from the work of a team of two business professors and the researcher, and a consensus was reached on each industry.

The final choices, *textile, mechanical engineering* and *electrical equipment and electronics*, were made by taking into account the following factors:

Would it be possible to find enough firms of comparable size?
Was it likely that firms in the sector would cooperate?
Were the sectors roughly comparable?

A sector was eliminated if either the firm size structure or penetration of foreign investments (many subsidiaries of foreign companies at the top of the list) was markedly different from the other sector.

PRACTICAL CHOICE OF POTENTIAL SAMPLE FIRMS

Companies must be local

The criterion which does most to distinguish the design chosen from the other possible designs is the requirement that companies must be local.

A company in the sample could not be partly (50 per cent) or wholly a subsidiary of a company of another country. However, a foreign company might have a 1 or 15 per cent interest; it was felt this would not have any significant bearing on control.

Companies must not be subsidiaries of larger groups of the same nationality

This criterion was used on the same grounds as the previous one. If a company is a subsidiary of another one, 'noise' in the management control practices may occur. (In one case, a firm which turned out to be a subsidiary was included in the study after it became clear that the parent company did not intervene.)

Some companies were partly owned by financial institutions or by banks, either as a result of direct investment or because a company had been in trouble. These companies were not excluded from the sample, as the usual consequence (for banks) was simply to have people on the board of directors and/or to choose the chief executive. The companies would not be compelled to adopt the bank's organisational style.

Product mix constant in a particular sector

Individual firms initially sampled were checked on the basis of the researcher's knowledge and of public documents. To eliminate those companies, apart from the researcher's knowledge of some companies, the basic source used was Dun and Bradstreet[3] which gives more details on products made and also gives for each firm a classification index (SIC). For German companies *Die Grossen Unternehmen in West Europa*[4] was also used as a check as it gives a three-digit classification of firms. Finally, for all public companies, for each country, a financial card was read to recheck products, addresses, names of chief executives, size and general financial background — *Extel financial analysis* cards for Great Britain,[5] DAFSA[6] for France and *Hoppenstadt Börsenführer*[7] for Germany. In Germany, it was not possible to obtain financial information for all companies, as many companies are private companies — family limited liability companies (or GmbH), and companies with full liability of owner (or KG).

Firms were eliminated when they were found to be unsuited to the sample guidelines. Some companies were too specialised in their product mix, and others turned out to be misclassified in the public sources used to draw the sample.

Companies must be of comparable size (as measured by sales)

For practical purposes, listings of companies in the three sectors were drawn according to the first two criteria (local, independent). They were then ranked by sales. (To select companies, *Le Nouvel Economiste*[8] was used. It ranks the first 500 French firms, then the first 5,000 French firms by sector, and also the first 1,000 in Europe by sector. The classification of *Le Nouvel Economiste* was checked for British firms by looking at *The Times 1,000*[9] which ranks by sales the first 1,000 British firms. Each firm however had to be checked individually to identify its sector. Both sources indicate whether firms are autonomous or are subsidiaries of larger local or foreign groups. For German firms, the main sources were *Die Grosste Fünf Hundert,*[10] *Wer Gehört zu Wem*[11] and *Textilwirtschaft.*[12]) Because the design did not allow for subsidiaries, it proved to be a difficult task to achieve comparable size from one sector to another and from one country to another. The degree of economic concentration in a particular country differed from one sector to another, as did the extent of multinational penetration.

Figure 3.1 gives the range within which firms were contacted and the range of sales within which they actually fell. Altogether fifty two firms agreed to cooperate in the study.

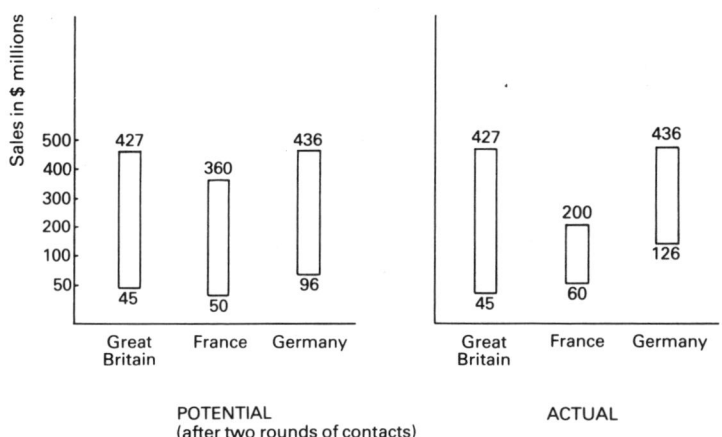

FIG. 3.1 Potential and actual range of companies in the three countries[13]

DATA COLLECTION

PERSONS INTERVIEWED

To answer the research question, it was decided that it would be necessary to interview four people in each firm, if possible: first the *chief executive*, second the *controller* and third one top manager responsible for *marketing* and one responsible for *production*.

In the case of the first interview,[13] there was no problem in identifying the person to whom to talk.

For the controller, only the head office controller was interviewed, even if he had correspondents in different units. (In France, *le Contrôleur de Gestion*; in Great Britain, the Financial Controller or Financial Director or Group Chief

Accountant; in Germany, the Head of Controlling, the *Betriebwirtschaft-Hauptabteilungsleiter* or *Abteilungsleiter*, or the head of *Rechnungswesen*.)

For marketing and production, the process of selecting one person in each field was more difficult. Usually this selection was made during the first appointment.

For one thing, marketing in most companies included in the sample means market research and analysis and not an operational responsibility for all marketing decisions (sales, price, promotion, product, distribution), which is a finding in itself. Some companies had marketing managers but they were the subordinates of sales managers. The researcher had to specify that he wanted a line manager and not a staff one. In most cases, operational marketing managers are called 'sales managers' in Great Britain, *'Directeur Commercial'* in France and *'Betrieb'* or *'Verkauf'* (sales) *'Geschäftsführer'* or *'Hauptabteilungsleiter'* (manager) in Germany. On only one occasion did an operational manager have the title of marketing director.

In the interview process it came about that, in fact, it was not easy to obtain for all companies the cooperation of four people. Certain chief executives refused to allow that managers other than themselves be interviewed, or just them and the controller. The difficulty may stem from the size of the companies. In all three countries, they are below the top one hundred in their country; they have been less used to outside investigations.

Certain firms were so ill-structured – a one-man show – that all functions of interest to the study were in their hands. On the other side, certain firms wanted more than four people to be interviewed to furnish a better idea (this happened mainly when there was a manager responsible for planning and another for control). At other times, the researcher decided that for production and sales it was better to interview a divisional general manager who would have a better grasp of the questions to be asked for production and marketing than to interview two people in his division. Finally, in certain firms the chief executive was not available, in which case I tried to interview somebody with a general management view who was as close to him as possible. (Vice-chairman or Managing Director in Great Britain, *Directeur Général Adjoint* or *Secrétaire Général* in France. In Germany, it was more difficult, especially in *Aktiengesellschaf-*

ten (either private or public) because they are all ruled by the European form of legal construction: there is first a council of surveillance (*Aufsichtsrat*) in which no executive is a member, and in which a third and soon a half of the members represent the workers. This council controls the executive management of the firm. Secondly there is a *Vorstand* responsible to the council which would correspond to the chief executive but the *Vorstand* has several members and sometimes does not have a chairman. Legally, the members of the *Vorstand* are supposed to take collective decisions. In practice[14] they often divide their responsibilities either by function (marketing, finance, production, personnel) or by divisions. In most cases, although he was not the person contacted, the *Vostand* member responsible for finance was the top management member who saw the researcher.)

With the preceding comments in view, the final number of persons interviewed by country and industry is as follows (Table 3.2).

HIGHLIGHTS ON THE DATA COLLECTION TOOLS USED

Overall presentation

The tools used to collect data consisted of interview guidelines about thirty pages long which have been used for all three countries. They were written in three languages and retranslated into French by the researcher to assure comparability. They were tested by interviewing managers prior to the study to ensure comprehension of the different questions.

The interview guidelines contain both quantitative and qualitative sections. In some areas, the researcher's objective has been to measure quantitatively the respondents' opinions. Many parts were open-ended, providing largely for qualitative comments.

A different guideline was used for each of the four different managerial positions. In addition to the responses collected from these interview guidelines, managers were asked to show and comment on their main control documents and related written materials. For the chief executive these consisted mainly of the annual report where available, the organisation chart, the

TABLE 3.2 Number of people interviewed

	France	Germany	Great Britain
Textile			
Chief executives	1	6	6
Controllers	–	6	6
Marketing managers	–	3	1
Production managers	–	4	1
Others[1 5]	–	5	4
Total	1	24	18
Mechanical Engineering			
Chief executives	7	7	8
Controllers	5	8	9
Marketing managers	4	6	9
Production managers	3	5	9
Others[1 5]	2	1	6
Total	21	27	41
Electronics			
Chief executives	5	3	3
Controllers	8	4	2
Marketing managers	6	1	0
Production managers	6	2	0
Others	2	1	2
Total	27	11	7
TOTAL	49	61	66

(Or a total of 175 persons interviewed).

regular reports he looks at (daily, weekly, monthly) and the planning manual. For the controller, the relevant documents were mainly the financial control budget forms and review of performance forms. For the marketing and production director, they were primarily his main control documents (regular reports) and organisation chart.

Wherever possible, all these documents, or sample representative forms (blank copies), were collected. Although those documents were blanks, the degree with which they were given varied from one firm to the other. In Great Britain, the degree of disclosure was the highest, closely followed by Germany. France came last. This may be a representation of the traditional

Research Design and Methodology 47

business secretiveness in France. Alternatively — the researcher being French — it could mean it is easier to do research in a foreign country, especially since secretiveness in Germany is generally considered to be worse than in France when companies are not public.

(b) *The interview process: methods and time requirements*

All interviews (175) were conducted by the researcher himself, in French, English or German, between December 1976 and August 1977. In Germany the researcher was accompanied by a translator in those companies where nobody spoke fluent English or French. This procedure was needed as the researcher understood German well but could not speak it fluently. It was felt that if the respondent answered in imperfect English or French, some information might be lost and that for certain technical vocabulary aspects it was better to have a translator.

The total length of time necessary to answer all questions for all guidelines and the comments on control documents varied from one firm to another. It ranged from 7 hours to 15 hours per company. Many companies and managers kept a copy of the guideline because they felt that it would be useful to have as a reference to think about their control system and certain problems they had not thought about before.

(c) *Content of interview guidelines: some highlights*

As already pointed out, management system variables and business variables affect control. Data have been collected not only on the dimensions of control described in Chapter 2 but also on structure, planning and to a lesser degree on leadership and objectives and strategies. Data on technology, markets and countries were collected mostly from secondary sources.

The questions asked to the chief executive dealt mainly with subjects elements and characteristics of control (mentioned in Chapter 2) from the top managers' viewpoint, such as:

1. His view of the control function (as distinct from other management responsibilities and not as a department).
2. The time he devotes to control.
3. What are the tools that help him monitor performance in

his firm (reporting and information systems) and what does he focus his attention on?
4. Factual data on the organisation structure, planning and leadership style.
5. His main objectives and the degree of success in achieving them. Most business and management system variables have been derived from the data collected from the chief executive.

The questions asked to the controller dealt mainly with the organisation of control and included:

1. the organisation of the control department and its functions;
2. his influence on control and his view of control;
3. the processes, formats, techniques, procedures and content of financial budgetary control and
4. the cost of financial control.

The questions asked to the marketing and production executives were identical; they dealt mainly with the characteristics of operations controls:

1. their view of control in their company and the time they devote to it;
2. the characteristics of control in production and/or marketing and
3. the control process in production and marketing for selected objectives (e.g., what standards are set; by whom; how and by whom is performance measured; with what frequency; who reports; about what and to whom; and who evaluates and takes corrective action?).

In addition, all interviewees were asked to assess the behavioral responses of people to control. This was used as a proxy, as the time, cost and priorities constraints of the research did not permit asking subordinates directly how they reacted to control.

Since several different persons were interviewed in each company and the interviewer typically had an opportunity to study company control documents between interviews, questions to clarify internal consistency were often raised.

SUMMARY

The priorities defined for this research in Chapter 1 and the subject matter developed in Chapter 2 have led to the consideration of several alternative designs. The design chosen consists of comparing three countries – France, Great Britain, Germany – and for each of them selecting comparable local independent companies in three sectors: textile, mechanical, engineering and electronics. A total of *fifty two companies*, about equally spread among sectors and countries, have cooperated in the study. In each company, where possible, *four* persons were interviewed. The *chief executive*, the *controller*, a *marketing director* and a *production director*. Each of them was interviewed by the researcher himself. Additionally, blank copies of the main *control documents* and related materials have been collected for analysis.

Part Two, which now follows, answers the first priority of this research by describing differences and similarities in the control practices of France, Great Britain and Germany; emphasising the chief executive's viewpoint, the controller's viewpoint and the operational viewpoint (marketing and production). As an introduction, Chapter 4 sets the stage by reporting the organisation and planning processes within which firms operate.

NOTES

1. J. Boddewyn, *Comparative Management and Marketing* (Glenview, Ill.: Scott, Foresman and Co., 1969), p. 2.
2. M. Haire, E. E. Ghiselli and L. W. Porter, *Managerial Thinking: an International Study* (New York: John Wiley and Sons, 1966).
3. *Principal International Business* (New York, Paris: Dun & Bradstreet, 1976).
4. *Die Grosse-Unternehmen Westeuropas*, Commerzbank (Damstadt: Verlag Hoppenstedt, 1976).
5. Extel Statistical Services, 37/45 Paul St, London, England.
6. DAFSA, Notices SER, 125 rue Montmartre, Paris, France.
7. *Hoppenstedt Börsenführer* (Damstadt: Verlag Hoppenstedt, April 1976).

8. 'Classement des 5,000 premières Sociétés Francaises et Européennes', *Le Nouvel Economiste* (Paris: France, December 1975, December 1976).
9. *The Times 1,000, 1976—1977* (London: Time Books, 1976).
10. *Die Grosse Fünf Hundert* (Luchterhand Verlag, 1976).
11. *Wer Gëhort Zu Wem?*, Commerzbank (Damstady: Verlag Hoppenstedt, 1977).
12. *Textil Wirtschaft*, no. 8 (24 Feb, 1977).
13. In France it is always the *Président Directeur Général* (chairman of the board and chief executive); in Great Britain, it can be the chairman, the chief executive or the managing director or the vice chairman and managing director. Many times when both chairmen and managing directors are mentioned, it means the chairman is not in an executive position. In that case, it is better to contact the managing director. In Germany, it is the *Geschäftsfürhrer* or *Geschäftsleiter* for KG and GmbH, and the *Vorsitzender des Vorstandes* — or the *Senior Vorstand* if there is no *Vorsitzender* — for an AG (chief executive or joint managing director).
14. F. Hoffman: *Entwicklung der Organizations Forschung zur Veberarbeirte und Erweiterte Aufgabe* (Wiesbaden, 1976).
15. Others include planning manager, division manager or managers who prefer to come in teams (two or three) for a particular interview.

Part Two

Describing Cross National Differences and Similarities

4 Management Processes: Structure and Planning

SCOPE OF CHAPTER

This chapter and the three chapters which follow will concentrate on presenting detailed descriptions of the differences and similarities in management practices between countries. As will be seen, there are sharp differences in control practices from country to country. These will be highlighted in Chapter 5 at the chief executive's level and elaborated in terms of the accompanying different ways of organising control in Chapter 6. Finally, in Chapter 7, the ensuing differences in practice at the operational level will be examined.

First, however, it is necessary to present the managerial context in which these patterned differences have their roots. The key features here are structure and planning. Management structure delineates the set-up in which firms operate. Several structural elements – such as the division of labour, means of coordination and degree of delegation of authority – were investigated in the fifty-two companies in the sample. There are significant differences in structural configurations from country to country.

As for planning, it has been defined as control's necessary counterpart – control is intended to ensure that performance conforms as nearly as practical to *plan*. The marked differences in approaches towards planning which emerge here from one country to another only serve to underline the importance of the link between the two functions.

Both features are described in detail in this chapter for each of the three countries investigated. The characteristics of structure will be presented first, followed by an account of the various conceptions of planning.

THE PROCESS OF ORGANISING

HIGHLIGHT ON BASIC MANAGEMENT STRUCTURE: AN OVERALL COMPARATIVE VIEW

Most companies studied in Great Britain are holding companies. A small central staff overlooks from twenty to fifty subsidiaries, each headed by a managing director, each having its own products, brands and markets and the necessary logistics to operate (administration, accounting personnel, etc.). Many decisions are decentralised to the subsidiary level and below, while the central office staff and directors shape policy decisions at the group level, act as bankers for the subsidiaries and monitor their performances. At the group level, as well as at the subsidiary level, top executives meet once a month to review performance and discuss policy matters. Usually a group executive chairs the local subsidiary committee. Such a structure allows for flexibility, autonomy of operations and entrepreneurship at the operational level, while orientation and monitoring are supplied by group executives and a small staff.

In German firms, the overall impression is one of 'hyper-specialisation', even at the top. Although half of the companies studied are organised by large *divisions*, the others are organised by functions. On the whole, one is impressed by the specialisation of management. The chief executive is in fact a *team*, in which each member has a functional specialisation; and, even in those firms organized by division, each division is headed by two or more functionally specialised executives. Central staff functions, support activities and services are quite extensive, providing assistance to local operations (functional and/or divisional) but also centralising a number of decisions (such as buying). Altogether, delegation of authority is low, much lower than in Great Britain.

Neat and well-compartmented as this structure is, executives are often called by their numbers which refer to the offices they hold. The top team will usually meet every week to coordinate functional specialisation. The overall impression is not one of flexibility but of operational efficiency.

Management Processes: Structure and Planning 55

In France, most companies have been found to be organised by functions. Central staff and services are as extensive as in Germany. Instead of choosing a divisional structure when activities are diversified at the operational level, chief executives prefer to head market or product commercial divisions responsible for the sales functions only, and product or geographical units for the production function. Many decisions are centralised at the top level, as in Germany, and committee management is scarce. The chief executive is often left with many final decisions when problems arise between functions.

This overall picture is now presented in a more detailed fashion on a per-country basis, more particularly shedding light upon the basic division of labour within firms, division of labour among top executives, role and importance of central staff, degree of delegation of authority and, finally, committee management.

THE BASIC DIVISION OF LABOUR

Table 4.1 shows large significant differences between countries. One could consider that both product—market and divisional organisations are similar except for legal differences. However, there are at least three major differences. First the division is usually larger in size than the product—market subsidiary. Secondly, there is no common central staff for subsidiaries, whereas one exists for divisions. Thirdly, there is very little interchange of men, money and material between product—market subsidiaries and each has its own brand name, which is not the case for a division. In France many groups have set up — for production or sales — different legal entities. They have still been classified as functional organisations, because they correspond only to legal and perhaps fiscal advantages but do not result in any difference in management behaviour from a pure — one legal entity — functional organisation.

The differences can be best described in detail by looking at the pattern of evolution of the different countries.

Excluding regional structure, the likely development of the British structure seems to be the following. As the size and/or diversification of the firm increases, holding companies regroup their subsidiaries into divisions and reinforce central staff. Chief executives' comments tend to characterise the likely develop-

TABLE 4.1 The basic organisation of labour

Number of firms	Great Britain	Germany	France
Organised by functions	1	8	12
Organised by divisions	4	6	3
Organised by product market subsidiaries	11	3	1
Organised by region	2	1	0
Total	18	18	16

(When comparing functional organisations to others which are profit centres.) $\chi^2 = 9$, df = 1, $\alpha = \cdot 001$

ment of the British structure as follows.

In its prime form, the structure is composed of wholly owned subsidiaries, each with its own board of directors, made up of the managing director and his immediate functional subordinates. They are loosely linked to a holding company. Headquarters comprises a financial director and a company secretary and a chairman. Group executives will usually be chairmen of each

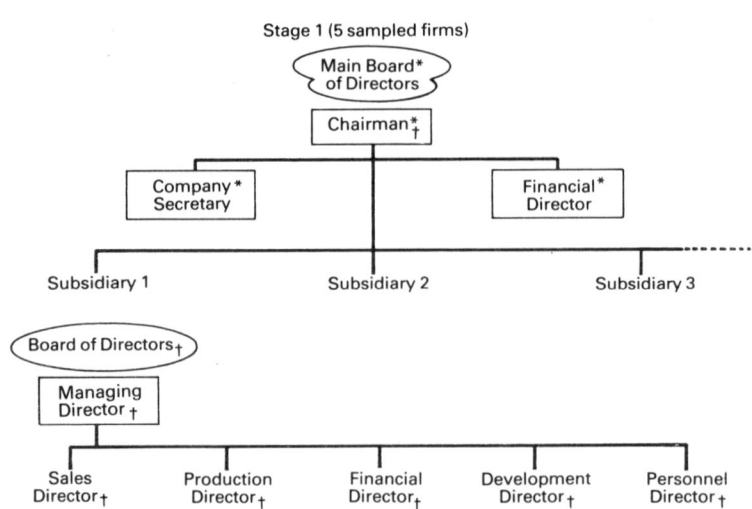

FIG. 4.1 The basic holding structure in Great Britain

Management Processes: Structure and Planning

individual subsidiary's board. (Structure seen in five firms are shown in figure 4.1).

When size and/or diversification increases, individual subsidiaries are regrouped into 'divisions'. These divisions are much more areas of interest than managerial centres. Each has a chairman — not always a full-time executive — who sits both on his subsidiaries' boards and on the main board. (Six sampled firms are shown in figure 4.2.)

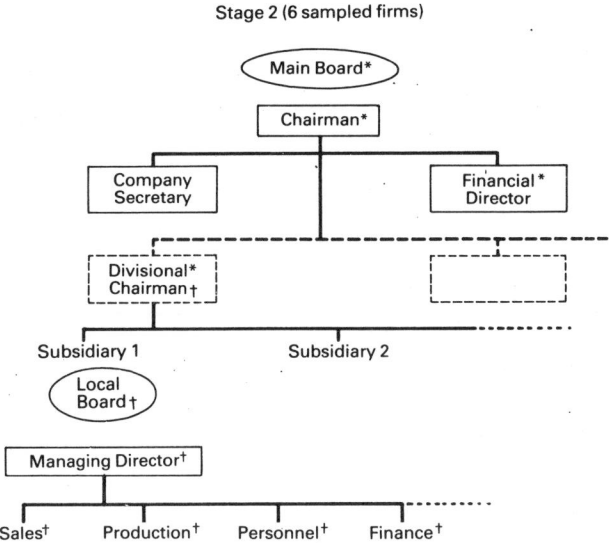

FIG. 4.2 The British holding structure with divisional domains

In order to consolidate diversification, the next step in this basic structure involves reinforcing central staff (group services, chief of planning ...), up to one hundred people. In addition, divisional chief executives become full time executives, and they also start to build a small divisional staff (three to five persons as financial, marketing, or technical advisors). The subsidiaries remain the basic product market unit. (Two sampled firms as in figure 4.3). Previous research[1,2,3,4] in the area of strategy and structure did not initially make a specific case of holding companies. Most of these studies were done from public documents (annual reports). Disclosure regulations oblige companies meeting certain standards to publish their sales by group (or divisions). This may have misled people to conclude that they were truly integrated divisional organisations as in stage 4 described here for British firms. An exception is provided in the comparative study of France and Germany by G. Dyas and H. Thanheiser.[5]

Finally, the full integrated divisional structure, seen in only two companies, involves larger divisions organised by functions

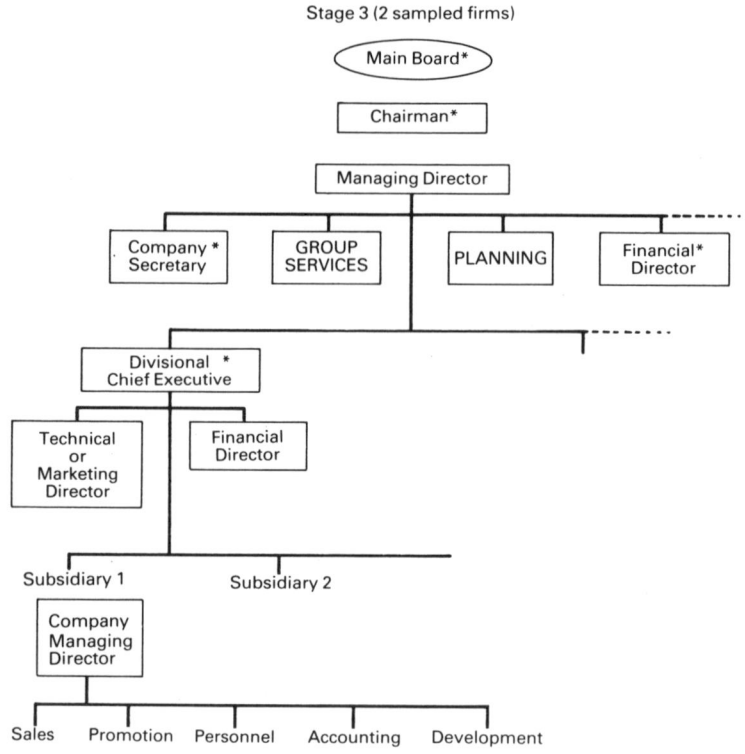

FIG. 4.3 The British holding structure with divisions

Management Processes: Structure and Planning

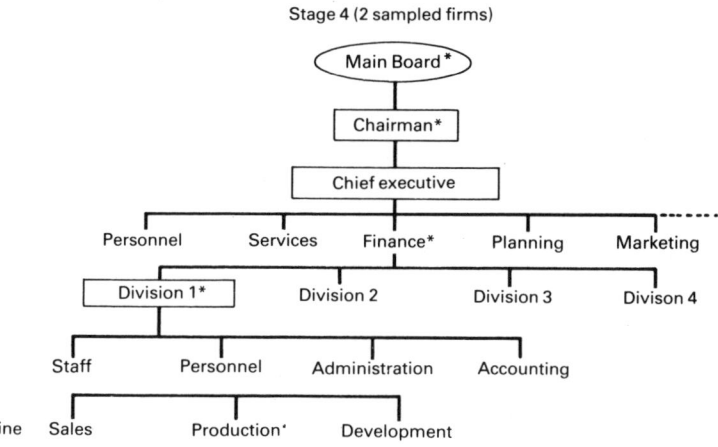

FIG. 4.4 The British pure divisional structure

for which central staff increases in size (over two hundred people). (See figure 4.4).

In Germany, the basic structure is either functional or divisional. Functionalism goes usually as high as top management. Whether the company is private or public, limited or unlimited, it will be headed by two to six equally responsible chief executives ('*Vorstand mitglieder*' or '*Geschäftsführer*'). Production and sales are always present, also finance and administration in most cases, followed by development and purchase.

In most cases each member of the top team will have all central services (or staff) and line managers related to his function reporting directly to him (i.e. no marketing or production general manager) (see figure 4.5).

The change from this functional organisation to a divisional structure does not seem, within the sample firms, to be induced by increase in size. Smaller as well as bigger firms may alternatively be functional or divisional. Diversification however may have some influence on the organisational settings. Divisional structures in Germany are much more integrated than their counterparts in Great Britain both at the headquarters level (more functions and people) and at the divisional level (central services and staff), with two possible arrangements at divisional

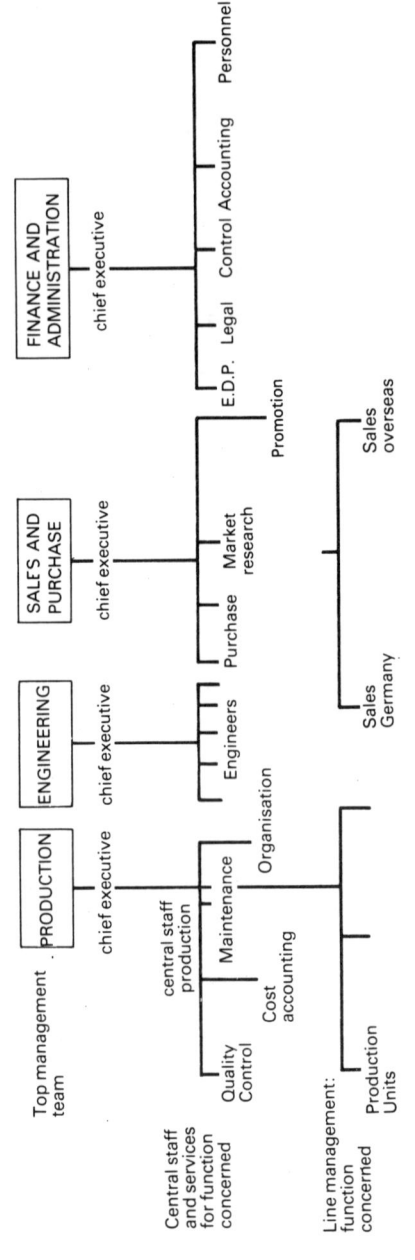

Fig. 4.5 The German functional organisation

Management Processes: Structure and Planning

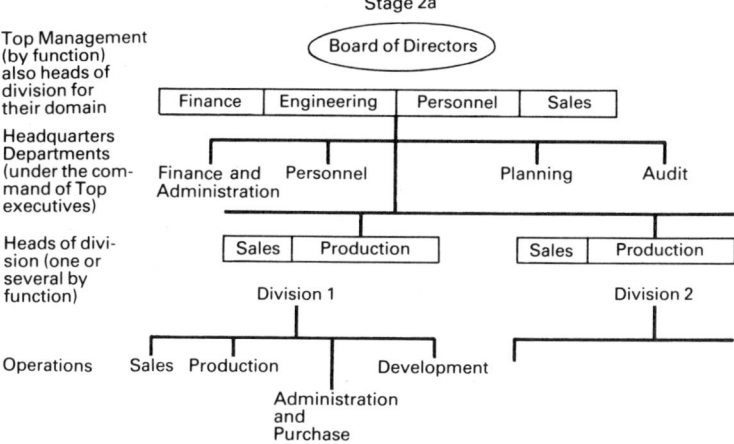

FIG. 4.6 The German divisional structure, type A

level – either one level of divisions or two (subdivisions) (figures 4.6 and 4.7).

In France, twelve of the sixteen companies are organised by functions. When the firm gets bigger and more diversified, however, there is a tendency to specialise production, and, even more, marketing by product types or groups, each one being

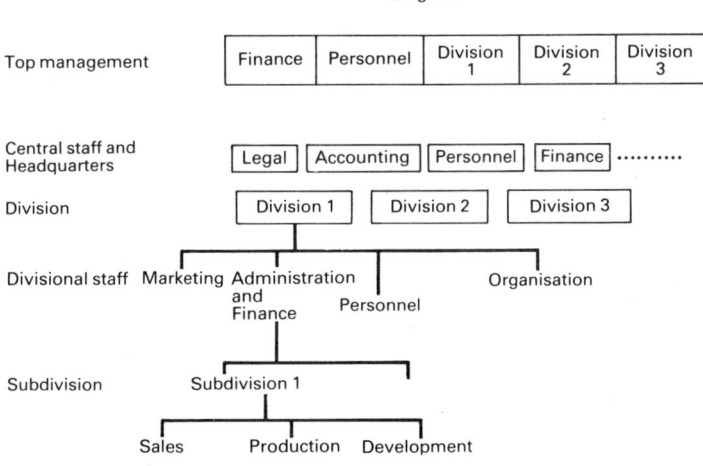

FIG. 4.7 The German divisional structure, type B

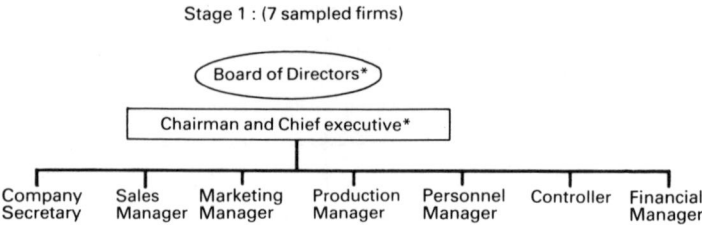

FIG. 4.8 The French functional organisation

headed by a manager who directly reports to the chief executive. In this structure, market and manufacturing units may be considered as profit centres, but still are functionally oriented. Central headquarters staff remains heavy and some decisions, such as purchasing, remain centralised (see figures 4.8 and 4.9).

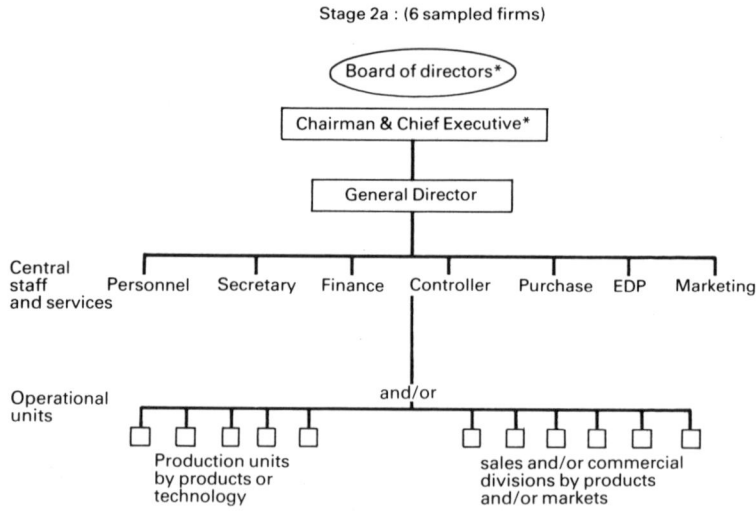

FIG. 4.9 The French functional structure, split operational

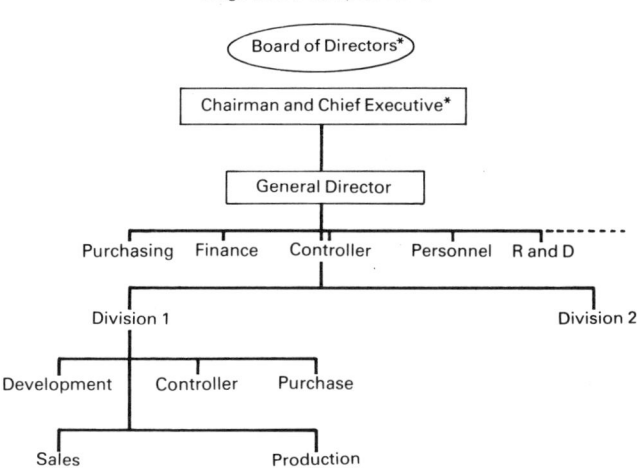

FIG. 4.10 The French divisional structure

Seen only in two cases, it does not seem that the divisional structure with its own production and marketing units is a matter of *size*, but rather a matter of management philosophy (e.g., a willingness by top management to decentralise and delegate — see figure 4.10).

DIVISION OF LABOUR WITHIN THE TOP MANAGEMENT TEAM

What is considered top management across cultures is difficult to delineate. It is defined here as those senior executives who deal with policy decisions and belong to the management committee which has been described as the highest in the company by chief executives.

Again and as a result of the previously described patterns, the orientation and division of labour among those top executives is different from one country to the other as shown in Table 4.2.

The top management meeting of the British organisation is in fact the main board meeting as, overall, an average of 69 per cent of board members are insiders — e.g., executives working in the organisation. Besides the chief executive and the financial

TABLE 4.2 Division of labour among top executives

	Great Britain	Germany	France
Mainly functional	6	12	13
Mainly divisional (or product markets)	10	3	1
Other (refers to regional managers mainly)	2	3	2
Total	18	18	16

$\chi^2 = 10\cdot42$, df = 2, $\alpha = \cdot01$

director, divisional chairman and/or chief executives participate in this meeting, bringing generalist viewpoints since they are specialised only with respect to the types of products and markets in their divisional area.

In Germany the top management group is composed of the members of the *'Vorstand'* or *'Geschäftsführung'* (an average of four people with such responsibility was found).

Interestingly enough, whether the structure is functional or divisional, top executives are most often specialised by function. In the latter case, for instance, the sales *'Vorstand'* member also serves as the sales divisional chief executive as shown in figure 4.11.

In France, it is more difficult to define who belongs to top management as many companies included in the sample look like 'one-man' shows. The chairman and chief executive (*'Président Directeur Général'*) is the only one to sit on the board of directors and, as most companies are functionally oriented, many decisions go up to his office. However, in cases where a top management committee is set up most of the people included in it will have a functional orientation with an over-

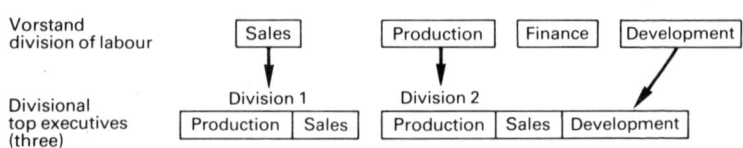

FIG. 4.11

representation of staff (as opposed to line) people: personnel manager, controller, financial manager, purchase manager, research manager.

CENTRAL STAFF AND SPAN OF CONTROL

Again, and as a natural consequence of the basic structure described at the beginning, there are differences in the total number of line directors or managers reporting directly to the chief executive (or team executive group in the case of Germany) and to the number of staff departments and people who report to the chief executive (see Table 4.3).

As the table shows, the British chief executive, helped by a light central staff and possibly three to six divisional chairmen, has to look over quite a large number of operational units. In fact, if the only functional organisation is excluded, the average number of headquarters staff people drops to fifty-four, from doorman to chief executive. Most staff will thus be found at subsidiary level and directed by an 'entrepreneurial' managing director.

TABLE 4.3 Staff and line

	Great Britain	Germany[a]	France
Average number of line[b] managers reporting to the chief executive	35	13	9.6
Average number of staff managers reporting to the chief executive	3.5	12	5
Average number of headquarters staff people for divisional, product-market and regional organisation structure	75	484	400[c]

[a] As there are four 'Vorstand' members on the average, only one fourth should be taken for staff and only half (sales and production) for line managers.
[b] For functional organisations, only sales and production managers have been labelled *line*.
[c] Only two such cases.

As for central staff directors — besides the mandatory company secretary and financial director — one may find a planning director with a staff of one to three people (seven firms have such a staff man), a director of personnel with a light staff dealing mainly with executive compensation and/or pensions (five companies have it) and, sometimes, a legal and patent director, a group services director dealing with buildings administration or internal consulting or EDP.

On the contrary, in Germany, one not only finds staff at the central level for divisional companies but also at the divisional level. At the central level, besides a very heavy finance and administration service (accounting, cost accounting, control, finance, taxation, legal etc.), one is likely to find almost everywhere an *organisation* department busy with projects to increase efficiency, a central personnel department and a central marketing department doing market analysis and research. The same tendency applies to France for the three divisional organisations.

DELEGATION OF AUTHORITY AND DECENTRALISATION OF DECISION-MAKING

The above description leads one to think that in France and Germany the tendency of firms to concentrate staff at the top — whether organised by divisions or functions — does not allow for much delegation of authority. On the other hand, the British structure — a mixture of corporate bankers and local entrepreneurs — should lead to more decentralisation of decision-making. The lack of central staff, which is good from a cost viewpoint, may also render it difficult to know operational matters in detail and thus does not permit too much centralisation. This was found to be the case (a scoring system was set up, based on chief executives' responses as to where in the organization seven types of decisions were made) as shown in Table 4.4.

Apart from major policy decisions (acquisitions, divestments, expansion) which are most likely reserved to top management, the British structure delegates most of the production, sales and personnel decisions to local subsidiaries as well as giving some leeway in the capital expenditures area. As one British chief executive said: 'The problem is to get good managing directors at subsidiary level and trust them.'

Management Processes: Structure and Planning

TABLE 4.4   Decentralisation scores by country

	Great Britain	Germany	France
Average decentralisation score	1.937	1.067	1.296
Standard deviation	0.55	0.392	0.610
Highest score	3.286	1.571	2.571
Lowest score	1.143	0.286	0.286
Range	2.143	1.286	2.286

France and Germany: t = 1.265, df = 29 ns.
France and Great Britain: t = 3.03, df = 28, α = .005
Germany and Great Britain: t = 5.25, df = 31, α = .005.

In Germany, the most decentralised decision under the top group and divisional managers is the one concerning the selection of personnel where the immediate superior has the final say on recruiting a subordinate. The same pattern is found in France, where additionally chief executives are often the only decision-makers in the areas investigated.

COMMITTEE MANAGEMENT

The frequency and number of top management level committees can attest to the coordination that is felt necessary to perform at top management level (see Table 4.5).

The need for more frequent top management committee meetings seems to go along with more functional specialisation (France and Germany). It is worth noting that three out of thirteen French companies do not feel that a top management

TABLE 4.5   Frequency of top management committee meetings

	Great Britain	Germany	France
No committee	1	1	3
Once a week	1	10	5
Once a month	15	5	5
Total	17	16	13

χ^2 = 12·22, df = 2 significant at α = ·001 for lines two and three.

committee is needed, thus reinforcing the idea of some 'one-man shows' going around in France. As for Germany, it is not surprising that the functional specialists think they have to meet quite often to integrate their viewpoints.

In Great Britain, as mentioned, in addition to the top management committee meeting, which is often the same as the main board meeting, each subsidiary has its own board composed exclusively of insiders (e.g., one group executive, the managing director of the subsidiary and his immediate functional subordinates). A group member is usually present in this subsidiary board to orally influence, probe and orient the subsidiary's performance and future. Additionally, but in a very limited number of cases (two), 'divisional' committee meetings are set up where the divisional chief executive or chairman meets with the managing directors of his area; this attests to the relative lack of relationships (or 'synergies') between subsidiaries. Moreover, the local board room is quite often the executive lunchroom where the managing director insists that his immediate subordinates eat with him every day. This gives an opportunity of meeting for coordination, and the divisional chairman will sometimes attend.

In Germany, the top management's weekly committee meeting is restricted to the members of the *Vorstand* or *Geschäftsführung*. This high frequency is deemed necessary because of the high specialisation of each member. Besides, various other committees meet once a month (80 per cent of the cases), either by function (sales people with sales *Vorstand* member, etc.) or by division, mostly to review performance as pictured by the following examples:

> 'As some units are production units and some others distribution units we have set up a product committee which itself is divided into three: product-distribution committee, product-research committee, product-production committee.' (German electronics firm.)

> 'Besides the weekly *Vorstand* meeting there is a divisional monthly committee meeting to review performance; the two managers responsible for a particular division will attend'

One area which serves coordination and on which the German company seems to be very keen is project management.

Management Processes: Structure and Planning 69

Various projects, mainly on rationalisation (i.e., aimed at increasing the productivity of a department, either a directly productive one (a workshop) or a service department, by rationalisation of methods with a specific quantitative target), circulate in the German organisation at all levels with specific tasks, timetables and objectives. A team of staff members (usually coming from the organisation or engineering and methods departments) usually assists an operational manager to attain rationalisation objectives.

When they meet, French top executives are mostly central staff. Other committees, when set up, meet monthly or quarterly but the purpose is for the general manager of a specific functional area and/or for the *'Président-Directeur-Général'* to give out information as illustrated in the following examples:

'He will see each of us separately (12 managers) in his office, at least once a month.' (French electrical equipment firm.)

'Every Monday the General Director, company secretary and factory managers meet; each time one of our four commercial managers attends to exchange information.' (French mechanical engineering firm.)

'For the year we have a schedule of technical meetings: each production unit will come and be seen by the chief executive individually.' (French electrical equipment firm.)

'Every month, on the 8th, all factory managers, the administration manager, all regional sales directors and international sales manager meet with the chief executive who gives out information and receives some.' (French electrical equipment firms.)

SUMMARY

Structural differences between countries may be summarised as in Table 4.6. This table, although mainly reflecting the researcher's impressions may fruitfully help the reader synthesising the major ideas previously developed. It highlights the many similarities which were found between France and Germany along with those countries' differences from Great Britain.

TABLE 4.6 Summary of differences and similarities in the structural characteristics present in the three countries

Major structural dimensions	Great Britain	Germany	France
Division of labour[a]	By product-market	By function or division	By function
Degree of decentralization[a]	High	Low	Low
Coordination by committee	High	Medium	Low
Top management[a] meeting frequency	Month	Week	Week
Amount of central staff	Low	High	High
Size of operational units	Small	Large	Large
Degree of specialization of top management	Low	High	High

[a] Quantitatively tested and found statistically significant.

THE CORPORATE LONG-RANGE PLANNING PROCESS

HIGHLIGHTS OF FINDINGS: A COMPARATIVE VIEW

Most British firms have been doing long-range planning for six years or more and many have set up special departments at the corporate level to collect individual plans coming from each subsidiary. Starting six months ahead of time – or even earlier – it is essentially a bottom-up process whereby each individual managing director submits a five-year plan every year which will be discussed individually at the corporate level, and then reshaped at the subsidiary level before being submitted again. An aggregate plan follows and is written before the budgetary sessions start. This process, which lasts about four to five months, involves about 100 people per firm, and planning procedures and content requirements are usually issued on a standard planning manual. The plan deals with all facets of the

Management Processes: Structure and Planning 71

unit and is not solely concerned with operations but is also strategic in nature.

Most German firms have also engaged in long-range planning but not for as long a time as the British ones. As in Great Britain, it is most of the time a bottom-up approach. The process usually starts a little bit later than in Great Britain (four months before its application), and people do not work on it for so extensive a period of time. Shorter in horizon (three years), it is much more orientated towards operations than towards strategy or strategic thinking. The only standard manuals that may exist focus upon financial forecasts. This happens all the more as quite frequently there is no separate department for long-range planning: the controller is responsible for both long-range planning budgeting and controlling at the corporate level. As a result of this organisation for planning, it sometimes happens that long-range plans are done together with, or even after, the budget or annual plan. Usually, fewer people than in Great Britain participate in it (70 people).

Less than half of the French companies engage in long-range planning. For those who do it, it often looks like three years' financial forecasting so as to look at what is coming rather than to take decisions today which can change the normal course of actions for tomorrow. The 1973 crisis seems to have disgusted some planners, and they have either stopped or become more suspicious about it. Thus, some firms have reduced the horizon (from five to two or three years), others abandoned planning altogether; finally two firms do it only every five years. Few people participate in the effort (50 people) and there is no planning manual to fix procedures or content requirements. As a result the effort is short (work on it lasts for two months) and half of the companies who do it prefer to do it after the budget.

These overall results are now illustrated and analysed in further detail to give a better feeling about the corporate planning process and highlight differences between countries. The characteristics of plans, the horizon, the organisation of planning, the content of plans and, finally, the planning process are now reviewed in turn more specifically.

THE USE OF CORPORATE LONG-RANGE PLANNING

Long-range planning has entered most British and German firms but not as many French ones, as shown in Table 4.7.

TABLE 4.7 Number of firms engaging in long-range planning

	Great Britain	Germany	France
Number of chief executives who report having a written long-range plan	13	14	5
Number of chief executives who do *not* have a written long-range plan	5	4	11
Total	18	18	16[a]

[a] $\chi^2 = 2 \cdot 98$, df = 1, significant at $\alpha = \cdot 10$, mixing columns one and two

The data indicate that long-range planning seems to have been ingrained in British management for a longer time period than in Germany or France, whatever the sector or size of companies. Because the planning has been going on for a longer period, or because the British are more confident about the accuracy of long-range projections, it also seems that the long-range plans have a longer horizon (over half British companies have five years plans vs less than a third for France and Germany).

THE ORGANISATION OF PLANNING

Details of the location of the planning department, when there is one within the organisation, reflects slight differences between countries in Table 4.8.

In the first case, a planning manager with one or two assistants reports to the financial director or to the controller who has also a budgetary control or cost accounting department. In the second case, the planning manager is likely to be directly responsible to the chief executive. In the third case, the controller is likely to be head of planning and control without specific departments for each of those tasks.

PLANNING CONTENT

The influence of these organisational arrangements upon planning content may be substantial. Indeed, if long-range planning

TABLE 4.8 Location of the planning department within[a] the structure

	Great Britain	Germany	France
Planning department separate from control department with different superiors	8	4	3
Planning department separate from control department under the same superior	1	3	1
Same department	4	7	3
Total	13	14	7[b]

[a] Cumulating rows two and three, vs row one, $\chi^2 = 2.98$, df = 1, significant at $\alpha = .10$ (after elimination of France). It is more common to find a separate planning department in Great Britain and more common to find planning and control in the same department in Germany.

[b] In this table and all following tables, seven French firms have been taken into account although two of them do a long-range plan every five years only.

is linked either directly (same person) or indirectly (through the same superior) to control, one is likely to find a much more quantitative, operational rather than strategic, type of planning — which is just what was found.

In fact, three sets of data indicate long-range planning is somewhat more strategic in nature in Great Britain, while it is rather figure-orientated and operation-orientated in Germany and France.

First of all, when executives were asked what areas their firms' long-range plans covered eleven out of twelve British companies were found to include structure in the long-range plans, whereas only six out of fourteen did so in Germany and three out of seven in France.

Secondly, through the analysis of long-range planning manuals and discussions with chief executives, strategic considerations — or strategic thinking (e.g., environmental analysis, analysis of strengths and weaknesses, etc.) — seemed to appear less explicitly in German and French firms than in British ones.

One question asked of chief executives was: 'What do you consider as the main critical factors for success in your business?'

TABLE 4.9 Number of firms for which long-range plans include structure[a]

	Great Britain	Germany	France
Long range plans include structural modifications if any	11	6	3
Do not include these modifications	1	8	4
Total	12	14	7

Fisher p = ·001

[a] The bloc France and Germany compared to Great Britain.

Typical answers obtained in the three countries confirm a marked difference between countries. The British chief executive tries to assess the distinctive competences one should have to succeed in a particular business, thus demonstrating that some strategic thinking has been somehow carried out in the long-range plans and he is not surprised by the question. The German chief executive is often first puzzled by the question and does not always understand it. It sometimes had to be asked twice. The answer relates more to what the company does, than to any outside evaluation of critical factors for success. The French chief executive is very trivial in his answer: price, quality and delivery whatever the sector, whatever the market segments, which would lead one to suppose that strategic thinking has not gone very far, at least explicitly, and has not resulted in any written document on the matter.

As a third indication of the strategic nature of long-range planning in Great Britain, it was found that more British firms have planning manuals. The planning manual does not only specify the procedures to be followed by units but also includes the types of questions which planners should ask themselves when doing the plan. If qualitative questions — such as definition of one's business, strengths and weaknesses, competitive advantages, etc. — are not required before arriving at a definite plan, then no manual is needed, just financial forms. Table 4.10 states how many firms in each country have such a manual.

Management Processes: Structure and Planning

TABLE 4.10 Number of firms having a planning manual

	Great Britain	Germany	France
Has a planning manual	10	7	0
Does not have a planning manual	2	7	7
Total	12	14	7

Fisher $p < \cdot 001$

For those French, German and British firms which do not have such a manual, the plan is likely to be just three or four or five years of income-statement forecasts.

However, the above tendency must not give the impression that such a thing as *corporate* strategy is better explicated in Great Britain. The role of the central planning staff and the planning process are such that in fact corporate strategy is often a mere aggregation of unit strategies.

THE PLANNING PROCESS

Whatever the country, the long-range planning in the sample firms (see Table 4.11) was found to be a bottom-up approach (apart from a few exceptions), which attests to the relative lack

TABLE 4.11 Approach to long-range planning

	Great Britain	Germany	France
Top-bottom approach with specific objectives given by top management to units	4	5	1
Bottom-up approach e.g. aggregation of unit plans	5	7	6
Bottom-up approach with some environmental assumptions given from the top	3	2	0
Total	12	14	7

of corporate strategic thinking (as opposed to unit strategic thinking), even for Great Britain.

This means that for many companies, except for some standard environmental assumptions which are sent to the units — such as prices of raw materials, wages increases, exchange rates, world economy — no additional pressures and constraints are given *a priori*. Of course, they are orally spelled out when individual plans are discussed in their first draft form. Because of the higher degree of strategic thinkings at product market unit level, eleven out of thirteen British firms start the planning process at least six months before its application. Each subsidiary prepares its plan and at *least one round* of discussion takes place before it is accepted. It is then approved two months before its application. An aggregate plan is prepared with additional corporate inputs (financing, for instance). This aggregate plan is ultimately presented to the board.

In almost all cases — ten out of thirteen — the long-range planning cycle is over before the budgeting cycle starts (see Chapter 6 for details). The plan involves the chief executive, the planner, the financial director, divisional chief executives or chairmen, managing directors of each unit with one or several of his immediate subordinates, and an average of approximately 100 people participate, at least to some extent.

In Germany, the planning cycle starts later on (three to five months before application) and worked for a shorter time, maybe because it is more figure-orientated. Sales, then production, then other functions give their intentions for the future which are then aggregated as a corporate or divisional plan. Less people (50 to 60) are likely to participate. Some companies in fact build the long-range plan together with the budget (three out of fourteen) or even after (five out of fourteen).

In France, data are scarce; the tendency is also for a functional approach with an aggregation at the top. Four companies out of seven cover only financial forecasting (e.g., forecasts of balance sheet and income statement) and even fewer people (30 to 50) participate in the process to some extent. Two companies abandoned long-range planning after 1973 and two others have reduced the horizon from five to three years. As one executive of a firm of 7000 employees commented:

> Those who say they do it and it works are liars. Long-range planning is an imbecility. Everything can change tomorrow.

Another one:

The crisis has showed us the uselessness of long-range plans. The performance did not come out the way it was planned. If you don't have some sort of reliability people get discouraged. It is better to reduce the horizon and have some kind of trust in the figures.

A third one (8000 people):

There is only a one-year forecast; we had tried in 1973 to do long-range planning. It did not create any mass enthusiasm. So we have settled for a one-year forecast and one person has been recruited to think about new products.

Finally, a general manager of a 6000-employee firm commented:

We do not have any formal long-term plan. Anyway the crisis has made us solve immediate priorities. The President General Director has some ideas of acquisition but he is very reserved, not explicit and not inclined to allow others to participate.

As a final description of planning, it is interesting to describe briefly an aspect of the one-year planning system which is detailed in Chapter 6. This aspect concerns mainly the difference in participation which appears between Germany on the one hand and Great Britain and France on the other. In Germany, there seems to be a very high degree of participation in the one-year planning cycle (or budget): every group of ten people or so is considered as a cost centre and will forecast its costs for the year. These objectives serve as a basis for monitoring each centre's performance from central headquarters. There seem to be less of that deep, detailed one-year planning in Great Britain. In France several companies divide the organisation into a certain number of cost centres, but often the forecast is done by the controller!

In addition, in Germany, management seems to require more that specific tasks and targets be set besides budgets. Some companies do not call the annual cycle a budget but a plan. They mean that it is not only a matter of financial targets but also of specific tasks that a department or an individual commits himself to achieve. Dividing specific tasks into subtasks, naming the persons responsible and forecasting dates of completion are planned as shown in Figure 4.12

FIG. 4.12   Simplified example of target-setting in Germany

Objective	Subtasks	Persons responsible	Date of completion
To increase machine A's efficiency and reduce cost by 5 %	Analysis of time Analysis of methods	....	....
To reorganise department B in order to achieve better coordination with sales	....	....	....

SUMMARY

It has been necessary to describe management structure and planning to provide a grasp of the framework in which control is achieved.

The basic organisation structure, the degree of decentralisation, the division of labour of top management and the size and uses of central staff have been investigated to lay out part of this background. The use, content, horizon, subjects, process and organisation of planning have also been described to give a clear understanding of the main management processes.

Certain key differences among countries appeared in both areas. To the extent that management processes are coherent, it appears that control practices are also likely to vary on a country to country basis.

As for structure, the British firms operate mostly as holding companies, leaving much autonomy to self-sustaining operating units; few exchanges if any occur between those units which are bound financially to the holding company. As a consequence for control, such a decentralised and non-synergistic structure is bound to lead to overall financial control rather than detailed or operational control.

Management Processes: Structure and Planning

In Germany, where companies are organised by functions or divisions, one is impressed by the high degree of specialisation all the way through. In return, the degree of decentralisation is much lower than in Great Britain. Those two factors should lead to a much tighter operational control from the top, all the more so in that top management is composed of several members who each have control of a specialised domain.

In France, the structure is overwhelmingly by function and many decisions are taken by the chief executive, acting alone. The pattern here, which gives the impression of differing from the high formalism and clear departmentalisation found in Germany, would lead to control which is less formal and systematic but which goes as much into operational matters as in Germany.

The fact that in Germany and Great Britain companies are more used to long-range planning than in France (although there is not any clear evidence of corporate strategic planning) would tend to make one think of a closer link between planning and control in those two countries (e.g., a control more orientated towards corrective action).

Finally, in Germany short-range plans go very deeply into specifying the detailed tasks to be achieved which would lead one to expect that control follows a similar pattern.

In the next three chapters control practices are described and references will be made to links with organising and planning processes where possible relationships exist.

NOTES

1. L. Wrigley, 'Divisional Autonomy and Diversification', Doctoral thesis (Boston: Harvard University, Graduate School of Business Administration, 1971).
2. R. Scott, 'The Industrial State: Old Myths and New Realities', *Harvard Business Review* (March–April 1973) pp. 133–48.
3. R. P. Rumelt, *Strategy, Structure and Economic Performance* (Harvard Business School, Division of Research, 1974).
4. D. F. Channon, *The Strategy and Structure of British Enterprise* (London: Macmillan, 1973).
5. G. P. Dyas and H. T. Thanheiser, *The Emerging European Enterprise* (London: Macmillan, 1973).

5 Management Control: The Chief Executive's Viewpoint

Since a major focus of the study is on top management control practices, the chief executive's conception of control is a natural place to begin our examination of control. A variety of dimensions are examined: what the chief executive sees as the main objectives of control, what emphasis he gives to the different functions of the firm, what information and reports he receives and pays attention to, and when and how he exerts control. Responses on these items provide a useful initial overview of the different dimensions of the control system outlined in Chapter 2.

As with structure and planning, the data show a number of sharp differences across countries. Attention will be paid to relations between differences in the view of control and the differences in structure and planning noted in the preceding chapter. Finally, some indicators of management control effectiveness will be noted and discussed in the light of the patterns which have emerged.

MANAGEMENT CONTROL OBJECTIVES PURSUED BY CHIEF EXECUTIVES

Control can have different meanings and objectives depending on how it is used in a particular company. Although it was defined as the process by which one ensures that actual performance conforms as nearly as practical to plan, one goal of the research was to check whether this was in fact how it was used

Management Control: Chief Executive's Viewpoint 81

in the different countries and how managers thought it should be used. Twelve questions were asked to describe chief executives' views of control as it is and as it should be. These questions covered three dimensions or orientations of control: one orientation focused on the cybernetic view of control (i.e., to ensure that actual performance conforms as nearly as practical to plan and take corrective action); another view focused on control as an instrument designed to police operations, to watch what is done; finally, as a third orientation, questions were asked to see whether control is thought to be an instrument designed to motivate and induce behaviour.

In fact the data show that control as a guiding instrument is perceived differently; that control as a mean of policing operations is more widely used in France and Germany than in Great Britain. Finally the relationship between control and behaviour is low in all three countries.

CONTROL AS A MEANS OF ENSURING THAT PERFORMANCE IS AS NEAR AS PRACTICAL TO PLAN

First, the researcher wanted to see whether top managers think control is, or should be, made to ensure that performance is as near as practical to plan.

Four related questions were asked pertaining to this dimension: 'Control is to make sure that performance is near to plan'; 'That resources are used effectively', that 'It allows corrective action to be taken when performance is different from plan' and finally that 'It is used to improve the quality of objectives'.

Significant differences appeared between countries not only as to how control is used but also as to how it should be, as shown figure 5.1. This diagram and subsequent similar ones are

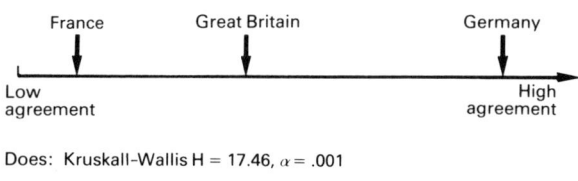

FIG. 5.1 Control does and should ensure that actual performance comes close to plan

meant only as useful visual aids for the reader instead of reporting scores for all individuals per country; it is not to be viewed as any kind of scaling of the 'distance' between countries, which would be mathematically improper. In this particular case, the result of the Kruskall—Wallis test only says that there is just a 1 per 1000 chance that the individuals would have come from the same population (e.g., no difference between countries), when it has been concluded that they do not (e.g., difference between countries). To draw this figure, the total ranks of individuals for one country were squared and divided by the number of individuals in that country. The highest number was found in France, the lowest in Germany (e.g., all German firms are grouped in first ranks), while Great Britain fell in between.

In Germany, the control systems appear to be much more stringent and oriented towards corrective action than in France and Great Britain. Regarding differences between Great Britain and France it is more a matter of degree.

In fact, in Germany at least one-year plans are much more detailed, not only in financial terms, but also in terms of individual projects and action programmes which are required from many people in the organisation (see comments on short-range planning sketched in the previous chapter). It is not surprising therefore to find control being used as a means of seeing whether those objectives (at least short term) are met. As an illustration Fig. 5.2 shows targets and performances for an eleven-person cost centre.

The profusion of detail that appear in this monthly report means not only that German companies have computers but also that they want to monitor performance closely for every tiny part of the organisation, so as to keep very closely to objectives and standards. As another example of this close link between planning and control, one German company has gone even further by setting up an exhaustive list of possible contingency corrective actions (*'massnahmen'*) and distributing it to managers in case part of the plan does not work. It is quite a massive document telling what possible actions can be taken: increase sales, decrease unit costs, etc.

The close link between planning and control was also expressed in the chief executives' comments:

> Control is to determine objectives, work on quantitative and

Management Control: Chief Executive's Viewpoint 83

qualitative planning as well as models, monitor results, analyse variances and work on corrective actions.

Control is all the actions which must be taken to direct the group based on the general philosophy written in the plan and budget: with the quantitative figures we ask what a man responsible for a unit will do to increase quality, productivity and organisation of work; they must take corrective action when performance differs from plan.

We go as far as defining standards and targets in terms of typing letters and the number of orders to be treated by one employee per day; the smallest unit (work place, machine group) will be a cost centre.

At the other extreme, many French chief executives do not see that the main task of control is to arrive as closely as possible to the plan. As one chief executive commented:

I do not feel control is made to ensure that actual performance is as close as practical to plan. I am very pleased in fact when performance is above what was set.

CONTROL AS A POLICING DEVICE FOR OPERATIONS

A second orientation of control may be its use for policing the operations by checking procedures, by getting as much information as possible, by looking over subordinates' shoulders to see if they make errors, by even trying to prevent those errors. These were the questions asked.

The analysis performed identified a significant trend shown in Fig. 5.3.

Pertaining to this dimension of control, the British chief executive does not think that control can be used to prevent subordinates' errors or see whether orders are carried out as defined. It is so much so that he does not believe that control should be used to give the boss as much information as possible. Answers in fact show that he would favour even less information arriving at the top.

In France and Germany, control used as a policing instrument is not just a matter of constraints that could arise because of lack of responsibility among subordinates; it is actually used in that way. The same questions asked about control — not as it exists but as it should be ideally — also gave the same significant differences between France and Germany on the one hand and Great Britain on the other. This view is coherent with the structural arrangements in France and Germany: a large central staff helps keep the boss informed, watch operations or even centralise some of them to avoid any mistakes. It is therefore not surprising that, later on, when the kind of information or reports the chief executive looks at are discussed, French and German executives report looking at more things more often than their British counterparts.

Management Control: Chief Executive's Viewpoint

FIG. 5.2 An example of an eleven-person cost centre in Germany

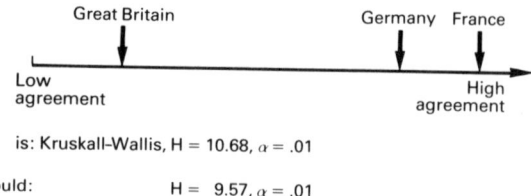

is: Kruskall-Wallis, H = 10.68, α = .01

Should: H = 9.57, α = .01

FIG. 5.3 Control used as a policing instrument

German chief executives commented as follows:

Control is to make available all information to management with respect to turnover, costs, personnel and weak points in the organisation and also to give recommendations to improve it.

If the boss is not informed, everything is random. It is the basis for everything.

CONTROL AS A MEANS FOR MOTIVATION AND INDUCEMENT OF BEHAVIOUR

A third dimension of control deals more specifically with the relationship between control and motivation, control and behaviour (see figure 5.4). The following questions were: Is control used to help evaluate a man's performance for rewards and/or punishment? Does it help managers to comply with organisationally desired behaviour or, on the contrary, is it meant for every individual to develop self controls? On this dimension, no significant differences appear between countries on the whole.

Although the differences among the three countries are far from striking the British seem to link personal evaluation and the results of control more closely, whereas it is less the case in France, and even less so in Germany. Does this mean that the

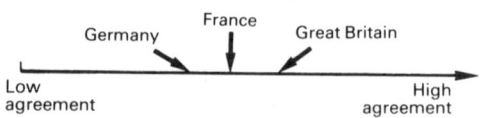

FIG. 5.4 Control used for motivating and inducing behaviour

Management Control; Chief Executive's Viewpoint

TABLE 5.1 Control helps a superior evaluate a subordinate performance for rewards and/or promotion

	Great Britain	Germany	France
Agree	14	4	8
Do not agree	4	11	7
Total	18	15	15

$\chi^2 = 10{:}3$, df = 2, significant at $\alpha = \cdot 01$,

British, who decentralise much more, must have an impersonal, quantitative way of evaluating performance for rewards and/or punishment and that compliance has to happen more by explicit mutual agreement to keep the organisation whole? Does it mean that, for instance, in Germany there is more an implicit assumption that everybody should perform well so that additional incentives are unnecessary? As for this last issue, one may more safely venture that the type of control used in Germany is not used as much as in France or Great Britain for rewards as shown in Table 5.1.

WHO IS IN CONTROL IN THE ORGANISATION

The objectives of control may differ according to who is responsible for control in the organisation. Marked differences appear between countries. British chief executives think that control is not specifically a task to be performed by top management, or even by top management and middle management only, but rather that control is everybody's task and responsibility and should be performed according to one's job. German and French chief executives do not think that control has to be distributed all the way through the organisation but that it should be concentrated at top and middle management levels (Table 5.2).

Table 5.2 suggests a number of comments.

(a) The British seem to have marked tendency to distribute control throughout the organisation, which is coherent with the higher degree of decentralisation previously perceived in British structures. Furthermore, they appear to be quite happy about

TABLE 5.2 Whose task is control?

Control is a top management task only

	Great Britain	France	Germany
Agree	3	7	8
Disagree	14	6	7
Total	17	13	15

$x^2 = 6\cdot2$, df = 2, $\alpha = \cdot05$

Control is everybody's task

	Great Britain	France	Germany
Agree	13	3	8
Disagree	4	10	7
Total	17	13	15

$x^2 = 14\cdot4$, df = 2, $\alpha = \cdot01$

the way control is distributed in the organisation as their views on the ideal patterns match the actual patterns quite closely.
(b) The French and Germans think that control is more concentrated at top and middle managerial levels than at lower levels, a view coherent with a lower degree of decentralisation as well as with a higher use of control for policing operations than in Great Britain.

However, when it comes to ideals, the French would love to give up some control at the top level and give it to lower levels in the hierarchy (eleven out of thirteen) which unfortunately – according to chief executives interviewed – is not yet possible in their organisations. However, it was not clear whether the reason for the discrepancy between actual and ideal views was due to the lack of potential among line, supervisory and blue-collar workers or whether the chief executive was afraid to delegate more and use less power from the top.
(c) The Germans seem to be the least inclined to leave control to subordinates (seven still think ideally it is a top management task only vs only three executives in France).

CONTROL INTENSITY OVER FUNCTIONS OF THE FIRM

Turning now to the functions of the firm which receive special attention at top managerial level, Table 5.3 demonstrates that the vast majority of chief executives do not give equal emphasis to all functions of the firm, whatever the country, although — whatever the country — they spend about 30 to 35 per cent of their time on control activities. Around this average of 35 per cent there are quite large variations. A look at the individual firms seem to indicate that those executives who spend a lot of time on control (more than 50 per cent) are either chief executives who overcentralise decisions or, alternatively, firms in which decisions, as well as planning, have been very decentralised.

In the former case, the chief executive wants to see that everything goes according to what he has decided — 'control as a policing instrument'. In the latter case, as planning as well as operational decision-making have been delegated, chief executives argue that their prime role is not to get involved in operations but to be aware early enough of something wrong.

Those who say they spend little time on control (less than 20 per cent) seem to be in all cases firms which have developed automatic formal control systems to such a point that they prefer to concentrate more on policy matters.

The fact that functions are not controlled with equal intensity is not surprising in itself. A particular strategic emphasis or particular functional emphasis, because of its overwhelming importance for success in a particular area, should be watched more closely.

TABLE 5.3   Are all functions of the firm controlled with equal weight?

	Great Britain	Germany	France
Control of all functions with equal intensity	3	4	3
Some functions are given more emphasis	14	12	12
Total	17	16	15

However, the ranks given by chief executives on the five main functions of the firm — production, finance, marketing, personnel and R & D — shows somewhat differing results between countries: finance comes overwhelmingly first in Great Britain, production comes first in Germany and France. Everybody agrees that personnel and R & D are less important. As for marketing there is no clear-cut pattern.

To test for difference between countries, a Kolmogorov–Smirnov two-sample test was applied two by two which showed a significant difference between finance in Great Britain and Germany ($\chi^2 = 9.99$, df = 2, significant at $\alpha = .01$); finance in Great Britain and France ($\chi^2 = 6.24$, df = 2, significant at $\alpha = .05$); production in Great Britain and Germany ($\chi^2 = 9.99$, df = 2, significant at $\alpha = .01$); production in Great Britain and France ($\chi^2 = 7.01$, df = 2, significant at $\alpha = .05$). All other differences in rankings from one country to the other were found not to be significant.

There is a consistently higher emphasis by British chief executives on controlling finance before any other functions. The nature of the British firms' structures may be a reason for it. A holding company with thirty or so subsidiaries needs a common denominator (in this case finance) as it may not be able to react significantly to operational matters (production, marketing, etc.) which are decentralised and geographically remote. The ranking of the other functions in Great Britain does not seem to be significantly different from one another, as shown in Table 5.4.

The emphasis on finance in British firms is further supported by chief executives' comments on their view of control:

> To control is how to maximise the use of resources: we control money supply, we look after the money.
>
> Top management control is more resource allocation. All except financial control is done at subsidiary level. When a problem arises, we ask what they are going to do about it and when; with thirty subsidiaries we cannot contribute to solve the problems.
>
> We would starve a company for money if they do not collect quickly enough.
>
> We do not try to control the way people operate but control

TABLE 5.4 Number of times British chief executives ranked the five functions in ranks 1, 2, 3, 4 and 5

Functions	Rank				
	1	2	3	4	5
Finance	13	0	0	0	0
Production	0	3	2	3	5
Marketing	0	4	3	1	5
Personnel	1	3	2	2	5
R & D	0	0	2	4	5

Friedman $\chi^2 r$ = 20·27, df = 4, α = ·01 all five functions
Friedman $\chi^2 r$ = 2·60, df = 3, n.s. when finance omitted

capital expenditures and borrowing. However, we are less ruthless than a U.S. corporation. We tend to back people longer.

In Germany, there are also significant differences between the functions' rankings as shown in Table 5.5.

This table seems to show that production and finance come more often at the highest ranks than the other functions. Personnel and research often come last in the ranking process, marketing being spread over the whole spectrum.

TABLE 5.5 Number of times German chief executives ranked the five functions in ranks 1, 2, 3, 4 and 5

Functions	Ranks				
	1	2	3	4	5
Production	4	4	5	0	0
Finance	5	2	2	4	0
Marketing	4	2	1	3	3
Personnel	0	2	6	3	2
Research	2	1	0	5	5

Friedman $\chi^2 r$ = 16·73, df = 4, α = ·015

Short-run planning and rationalisation programmes done under project management all emphasise production costs in Germany. As one executive joked about the difference between the German and the British:

> In Germany, when the Deutschmark goes up by 5 per cent we put action programmes to increase productivity by 6 per cent to stay competitive in international markets. If an Englishman would see the pound go up, he would say: let's have a drink.

The ranking of the five functions by French chief executives is close to that observed for Germany (Table 5.6 below).

Generally speaking French chief executives come from the technical side. This fact was also found in the sample firms. Such executives are naturally inclined to pay more attention to what they know best, which is production. However, finance comes very close. (Except for finance and production, which seem to be attributable to country differences, normatively one would think that a stronger relationship between control intensity and the sectors in which firms do business should exist. For instance in an unstable environment, where market changes are large and brisk, marketing should come first. Similarly, research and development should prevail in areas where complex and innovative technology is crucial. This latter relationship is left for full detailing in Part Three, after all

TABLE 5.6 Number of times French chief executives ranked the five functions in ranks 1, 2, 3, 4 and 5

Functions	Rank				
	1	2	3	4	5
Production	4	5	2	1	0
Finance	6	3	1	2	0
Marketing	2	4	1	3	2
Personnel	0	0	5	3	4
R & D	0	0	3	6	2

Friedman $\chi^2 r = 29$, df = 4, $\alpha = \cdot 001$

descriptive data concerning control have been presented. Surprising enough, for this particular aspect of control intensity, suffice it to say at this point that no statistically significant differences were found between sectors or any other variables except country.)

Up to this point, this chapter has first allowed us to look closely at the objectives pursued in control, as viewed by the chief executives. Those objectives were then translated into the chief executives' assessment of whose task control is – their evaluation of what importance the control function has. Finally, an explanation as to why certain control functions were favoured by certain executives was proposed. All these elements put together tended to indicate some differences between countries in several respects. French and German firms seem to be more production-orientated, more oriented towards control as a means of policing operations and more inclined to concentrate control at the top of the hierarchy. Coherent with their planning emphasis and low degree of decentralisation, this reveals quite a tough top management style, oriented towards operational efficiency and pyramidal organisational settings. The British seem to be more lenient and participative in their leadership style, more oriented towards financial matters and flexibility, leaning towards autonomy and self-control, feeling it better to stand as a trustee than a sentinel. Further confirmation and specification is needed to better apprehend those differences as well as to indicate what tools are used to fulfill those control objectives and philosophies. The following section describes in detail the type, frequency and use of information which chief executives look at; by giving examples of the specific tools and documents, the reader will be better able to visualise differences and similarities.

CONTENT FREQUENCY AND PROVISION OF TOP MANAGERS' REPORTS

OVERALL COMPARATIVE VIEW OF FINDINGS

Overall, the information or data that chief executives primarily look at are overwhelmingly internal. Except for one or two chief executives who mentioned looking daily at the stock exchange or currency rates, most executives look at information coming from inside of the organisation (such as sales, orders, deliveries, output, profit, cash, personnel, etc.).

Inward-looking as they are, they are also overwhelmingly interested in short-term performance as a monitoring device. A sometimes quite impressive and standardised reporting system, dealing with all aspects of the business performance, arrives on their desk every week or month. No evidence, except in one case, was found of some sort of strategic control.

Country differences indicate a sharp distinction between the British on the one side and the German on the other — French chief executives' monitoring tools falling in between, leaning towards the German ones, but with less systematisation, less automation and less rigour.

The British chief executive is less likely to look at daily or weekly information than his German or French counterpart. The information is likely to contain some outlook on future expected performance (for instance, on budgets it is likely that a special column would be set to show what is 'now expected to the end of the year'); some qualitative written report to highlight key results — the information supplied to him is likely to come directly from each managing director of the subsidiaries, thus bringing a low degree of participation of central staff. Finally, the content of the report is heavily oriented towards financial control. On the other side the German — and to a lesser degree the French — chief executives are likely to receive more frequent information, mostly based on past performance rather than the future; almost always quantitative, this information is likely to be less financial but more sales- and production-oriented. Central staff computes and supplies most of it and automation is required. Finally, as many companies are organised by functions, performance results do not always fit the structure (performance by product, market, etc.).

CONTENT OF REPORTS TO CHIEF EXECUTIVES

Strategic control — e.g., control set up to monitor the performance of a chosen strategy — is not used by chief executives. They rely more on monitoring short-term performance than on focusing their attention on critical factors for success or on evaluating distinctive competences. This is not surprising, as not many companies have developed corporate strategic planning

Management Control: Chief Executive's Viewpoint 95

or thinking. As a unique exception, a British company in the electronics sector has developed a control system to monitor what they consider a key factor for success: no equipment sold to a customer will be 'down' (i.e. out of operation) for more than twelve hours. To check on this, every morning and afternoon the chief executive is warned when an item of equipment has been down for more than twelve hours and corrective action is immediately taken at the highest level to replace or send a part or equipment to the customer. A systematic procedure has been set up whereby a service man unable to repair equipment within two hours notifies his superior, who in turn notifies his own superior after two more hours (and so on up to the chief executive) in order to allow close control over what has been defined as a distinctive competence by the company: no down time whatever the cost.

The monthly report is the prime basis for monitoring performance. Depending on the firm's desire to get more details and/or its wish to get more accuracy than speed, these monthly reports arrive between fifteen to forty-five days after the end of the month. Some chief executives use preliminary reports which give them the opportunity to have essential results, such as sales, orders or gross profit (even estimated) earlier (in three, four or five days). The degree of sophistication is variable within one country and from one country to the other. A few chief executives in fact have not set up sophisticated reporting systems; their management style is more orientated towards informal meetings with their executives, towards talk over the phone rather than full-fledged reports. Smaller firms tend to follow this pattern, especially family-owned enterprises, as well as many functional organisations.

Table 5.7 summarises the content of those monthly reports

As may be seen, the described emphasis on financial matters from British chief executives (unit balance sheets, receivables return on capital) is reinforced in the monthly report! It also shows the higher reliance of French and Germans on detailed costs, personnel and quantities produced.

FREQUENCY AND DEGREE OF DETAIL

Table 5.8 indicates that the British are less inclined to look at daily information than both of their counterparts.

TABLE 5.7 Number of companies in which the monthly report to the chief executive includes the following items (computed from a content analysis of documents)

Does the monthly report encompass:	Great Britain		Germany		France	
	no.	%	no.	%	no.	%
Outlook for the future (qualitative reports and/or projected figures.	12	67	4	22	6	37
Overall group Balance sheet	10	56	4	22	4	25
Unit balance sheet (subsidiary, division, subdivision)	13	72	2	11	0	0
Overall group income statement. Profit and loss statement	15	83	8	44	8	50
Unit income statement	18	100	17	94	13	81
Personnel statement (direct, indirect; ratios, etc. . . .)	10	56	15	83	11	73
Inventory ($)	15	83	15	83	14	93
Receivables	15	83	11	61	7	47
Orders	15	83	11	61	10	67
Return on capital	9	50	3	17	3	20
Capital expenditures	11	61	8	47	5	33
Detailed costs	5	28	18	100	14	93
Quantities produced	0	0	15	83	12	80

This seems coherent with the decentralization philosophy of British companies — control is not so much getting into operational matters and telling managers what to do. As one chief executive commented: 'We expect them to run their units without detailed direction'.

As a result, a further look at the responses and documents indicates that less information is likely to be consulted by those British who look at daily or weekly information (Table 5.9). A content analysis showed that seven items were present: sales, orders, production output, personnel, cash, mail and deliveries.

TABLE 5.8 Frequency of top manager's information

	Great Britain		Germany		France	
	no.	%	no.	%	no.	%
Number of chief executives[a] looking at daily information	5	20	12	67	8	53
Number of chief executives looking at weekly information	11	61	13	72	10	63
Number of chief executives looking at monthly information	18	100	18	100	16	100

[a] $\chi^2 = 5\cdot 97$, df = 2, $\alpha = \cdot 05$

Some chief executives look at one of these items only (e.g., sales), others at two of these, others at three, etc.

Also the British chief executive is less likely to receive and to look at the detailed cost or output figures. Only aggregated direct and fixed costs – sometimes broken down into labour and material direct costs, and manufacturing, marketing and overhead fixed costs – are provided (Table 5.10).

TABLE 5.9 Number of items looked at

	Great Britain	Germany	France
Average number of items looked at daily	1·8	2·4	2
Average number of items looked at weekly	1·8	2·8	2·4

TABLE 5.10 Number of monthly reports to chief executives which include detailed costs

	Great Britain	Germany	France
No detailed costs	13	0	1
Detailed costs	5	18	14
Total	18	18	15

Fisher p = ·001

A further look at the number of times each weekly item is looked at show that, for Great Britain and Germany, cash comes first. Afterwards the British emphasize the future more (orders) whereas the Germans emphasize the past (sales) and output (production, deliveries). The French are in between. This difference reinforces the policing orientation of German control and would suggest that information on past performance rather than warning systems are more common in Germany than in Great Britain. In one case (Germany), chief executives want to make sure they are informed of what is going on; in the other case (Great Britain), chief executives, who have delegated, want only to be warned of unusual matters.

CHARACTERISTICS OF INFORMATION SUPPLIED TO CHIEF EXECUTIVES

In fact, much data indicate that information supplied to the British chief executive is more a steering instrument, or early warning system, than for German and French executives.

For one thing, the British chief executive's report more often deals with the future than does the French or German.

Also, relatively more British companies than French or German ones receive a qualitative report (or reports) emphasising some large variations and venturing explanations of those variations.

As one German chief executive mentioned: 'We prefer to have all the facts; they speak for themselves. Otherwise you could get one million reasons why performance was not up to the plan.' Whereas one British chief executive said:

'We expect managing directors to emphasise variations from an agreed strategy and objective.'

It is also more likely that British chief executives will require – for the whole group as well as for every unit – reports on a certain number of items which are meant to highlight exceptions. Practically, it means a front page report which summarises key figures.

In addition, British chief executives occasionally get the minutes of the subsidiary board meetings to see what has been discussed.

To confirm the lower degree of quantification in the British control idea, whereas ten out of eighteen and nine out of sixteen French chief executives feel that the reports they get are entirely quantitative, only three out of eighteen feel this way in Great Britain ($\chi^2 = 6\cdot71$, df = 2, $\alpha = \cdot05$).

These results indicate a somewhat higher degree of management by exception by British managers, which is quite understandable when one thinks that each subsidiary's report will be looked at by the chief executive (except in divisional structures — and there may be thirty of them).

Based on interviews and analysis of documents, the Table 5.11 summarises these differences.

HOW DO THEY GET THOSE REPORTS?

The functional nature of many French and German companies makes it rather difficult to obtain reports from people responsible only for specific products and markets. Even in divisional structures, because of their relatively large size, performance is broken down by product groups. Thus reports have to be built up through information systems. The British structure, mainly including product-market subsidiaries, facilitates the reporting of business performance per product-market. It is not surprising, therefore, to find more French and German companies for which monthly reporting to the chief executive is prepared centrally rather than prepared by the units being reported on.

Typically, in Great Britain, all the quantitative elements of the management control (monthly accounts) will be filled out by the subsidiary managing director with the help of his chief accountant or financial director in a standard format. The managing directors highlight the main results in a two-page qualitative report and sign both the quantitative and qualitative reports. These are sent to the group financial director who does some consolidation (sales and profits by division, where applicable, group balance sheet and income statement) and sometimes a group qualitative report. The sum of all subsidiaries reports (ten pages each) and the financial director report is then presented to the chief executive and main board every month.

All companies insist that the managing director fills out the performance report by *hand* and signs it: no computer output is permissible. As one executive puts it: 'At least we know he has read it.' Even the financial director of one of the biggest

TABLE 5.11 Characteristics of information supplied to chief executives

Information supplied contains:	Great Britain	Germany	France	
Information supplied contains plan performance and now expected	9	4	3	$\chi^2 = 6\cdot48$, df = 2, $\alpha = \cdot05$
Written statement accompanies the quantitative report	12	6	6	$\chi^2 = 4\cdot87$, df = 1, $\alpha = \cdot05$
Key figures report	12	5	9	$\chi^2 = 5\cdot9$, df = 2, $\alpha = \cdot05$

(Great Britain 18 obs.; Germany 18 obs; France 16 obs.)

Management Control: Chief Executive's Viewpoint

TABLE 5.12 Who prepares the reports sent to the chief executives?

	Great Britain	Germany	France
Prepared centrally	1	12	11
Prepared locally with or without some central consolidation	17	6	5
Total	18	18	16

$\chi^2 = 15 \cdot 3$, df = 2, $\alpha = \cdot 001$

British European computer firms mentioned: 'They do it by hand, the computer is not reliable.'

By this he meant, as other chief executives did, that he wants to make sure that the managing directors feel responsible and accountable for their performance as well as projections to the year's end. Chief executives do not want those performance figures to be computed centrally and then handed to the subsidiaries, or left in the hands of accountants.

The Germans and the French — more systematically and in more detail for the former — will have performance computed centrally, with heavy help from mechanical devices. The computer programs are quite integrated, giving all results in fiscal accounting, cost accounting and control, in many cases by product. All kinds of analyses can be made. Not only performance is reported in financial terms but also output and personnel. Even if the computer is not involved, results are computed centrally more often than not.

SOME INDICATIONS OF TOP MANAGEMENT CONTROL EFFECTIVENESS

Given these top management control practices, one may wonder about the effectiveness achieved in each country.

As defined in this research the objective of control is to ensure that performance is as near as practical to plan. Thus if one objective is set at 100, control is the most effective when performance equals 100. Chief executives were asked to give their evaluation or the figures of achievement as compared to

TABLE 5.13 Average degree of achievement of five most important objectives in last year

	Great Britain	Germany	France
Average	85·5%	90%	77.2%
Standard deviation	10·65	9·6	17.6

Germany and France: t = 2·55, df = 14, α = ·025
Great Britain and France: t = 1·52, df = 16, α = ·07

this 100 base. Our definition, of course, insists that being 20 per cent over objective is just as ineffective as being 20 per cent under objective. Chief executives were asked to state their five most important objectives over the last five years, and the corresponding yearly performance (to test for consistency over time): however, in most companies only last year's performances could be obtained and are reported in Table 5.13.

Table 5.13 suggests that the French seem to be much less effective in coming near to plan than the British and the Germans; there is also a wider variation around the average in France, some executives mentioned having achieved 40 per cent or 160 per cent of objectives for a particular year! The researcher's impression, somewhat substantiated when correlating effectiveness and sophistication in planning, is that the wide discrepancy between objectives and performance is in fact due to the lack of *planning*. In other words: the less planning, the less control (at least as a guiding instrument). On the contrary, although German and British offer quite different control principles, they seem to be as effective in their corresponding philosophy and context.

SUMMARY

This chapter has emphasised the objectives, means and tools used by chief executives to control their businesses. For the particular sectors and sizes of enterprises under study, certain national patterns have emerged. These tendencies are summarised in Table 5.14 in terms of the key characteristics of top management control.

Table 5.14 Summary of the tendencies of key characteristics differentiating countries with respect to top management control[a]

	Great Britain	Germany	France
Control as a consequence of planning	Low	High	Low
Control as a motivation	High	Low	High
Control as police	Low	High	High
Finance oriented	High	Medium	Medium
Production oriented	Low	High	High
Marketing oriented	Medium	Medium	Medium
Evenly distributed through the organisation	Yes	No	No
Degree of detail	Overall	Very detailed	Detailed
Orientation	Future	Past	Past
Qualitative or quantitative	Some qualitative	Quantitative	Quantitative
Frequency	Month	Week	Week
Prepared centrally	Low	High	High
Degree of systematisation and standardisation	High	High	Low

[a] High and low are only meant in relative terms: a more proper way would be to state 'higher' and 'lower'.

This table indicates a less detailed and less operational control from the top in Great Britain and a higher emphasis on financial control, which is coherent with the type of structure developed in British firms in which operational autonomy and flexibility are favoured.

This type of arrangement would appear to require – and depend more upon – a broadly defined planning process to define performance criteria and on early warning systems to avoid surprises. As a result, the British system of control seems to demand more management by exception, more highlighting of deviations, as well as some figures to project future performance.

In Germany, it is more or less the opposite. Systematic and methodic and detailed operational control reach the top. Coherent with the systematisation of structure and the high degree of detail in one-year planning, controls are orientated towards operational efficiency to reach specific quantitative targets. As a consequence, information is detailed, quantitative and prepared centrally.

France seems to be in between, leaning towards the German style but with less emphasis on systematisation, perhaps because of a lack of detailed planning. In terms of control effectiveness there does not seem to be sharp differences between the German and British samples although the practices are different. However, both countries differ significantly in that respect from France where performance diverges widely from plans.

A certain number of similarities in chief executives' views of control also appeared. Strategic control — set up to monitor the performance of a chosen strategy — is not employed much by any of the chief executives. They rely more on monitoring short-term performance than on focusing their attention on critical factors for success or on evaluating distinctive competences. This is not surprising, as few companies have developed corporate strategic thinking.

As another similarity, control is very much viewed and used as an impersonal formal process rather than a method of inducing individual motivation and behaviour. This may be due to the nature of European values whereby performance is much less viewed in terms of economic achievement only and people are perhaps less motivated by the work ethic or a 'fair day's pay for a fair day's work'.

Also, many top managers do not think that control is something that should cover all aspects of the business. They prefer to emphasise specific aspects or functions. In turn, however, the particular emphasis given appeared to vary by country: finance is stressed more in Great Britain, production in France and Germany.

Continuing the description of cross-national differences and similarities in control practices the next chapter approaches these differences and similarities from a different angle: the organisation of the control system, particularly from the perspective of its contribution to chief executive control.

6 Top Management – The Controllership Function

SCOPE OF CHAPTER

This chapter refines differences and similarities in top management control by looking at the organisation and function of the control departments. It has been selected for several reasons. As a specific department it gives a fair representation of the formal systems at work – at least in the financial area within which the basic top management reporting systems are designed and worked out. It thus provides additional data on the formal ways (documents, processes, methods) in which control is practiced. Furthermore, from the top management point of view, the control department – as a staff function – is often the privileged location for collecting and analysing performance. Thus it can shed light on the way chief executives monitor performance by looking how information is collected to be given to chief executives.

Finally the control department can also be the main instigator of methods and procedures in operations control and a prime link between headquarters and operations. By describing its role influence and systems design it helps to understand and predict probable consequences for operations controls, which will be viewed in the next chapter.

The information analysed in this chapter essentially comes from interviews with the headquarters' controller in each company as well as an analysis of the formal control systems (reports prepared for chief executives, accounting methods).

After having presented the control departments, the data bases assembled by these departments are discussed. Emphasis is given to implications for top management profit control and budgetary control.

CONTROLLERS' OBJECTIVES PURSUED IN CONTROL

An analysis of responses to the same questions on the objectives of control as the ones asked to chief executives show the same emphasis in each country. No wide differences appear for a particular country between the controllers as a whole and their bosses except for one country — i.e., the use of control as a policing instrument in Great Britain.

This reinforces the idea of national differences which were tentatively explained in the previous chapter by the differential degree of delegation among the three countries and the different focuses on planning: in Germany for instance, where decisions were found to be centralised and planning quite detailed, the use of control both as a policing instrument and a monitoring device for plans seems also to be the view of the German controllers.

This structural interpretation of the close general agreement between chief executives and controllers is also confirmed by the fact that, whatever the country, in about 80 per cent of cases the chief executive decides what he wants from the control department.

The only systematic difference noted between controllers and their bosses was found in Great Britain. British controllers emphasise one aspect of control — ensuring that procedures are precisely followed by subordinates — more strongly than their superiors. This particular emphasis on their part is quite under-

TABLE 6.1 Differences in views: chief executives and controllers[a]

	Great Britain	Germany	France
Control as a consequence of planning	No difference	No difference	No difference
Control as a policing instrument	Significant difference	No difference	No difference
Control as a tool for motivation and behaviour	No difference	No difference	No difference

[a] To test potential differences, a Mann—Whitney U Test was used: for each factor, the controllers' and chief executives' scores were ranked ($p < .001$)

Top Management—The Controllership Function 107

standable. They design management control systems which generally result in standard formats for monitoring performance. They are often geographically far from operational product-market units. Moreover, performance measurement is directly done by operational units. As a result, they want to make sure that the measures used in those monitoring devices are comparable and trustworthy throughout the system (e.g., accounting procedures, methods of aggregation, methods of calculation, as well as for instance cash remittance procedures). The highest priority from the group point of view is thus to have a sound information system as a basis for control. This aspect of management may, in fact, be one of the main synergistic effects which may be expected from decentralised holding organisations.

THE FUNCTIONS OF CONTROL DEPARTMENTS: THEIR LOCATION, SIZE AND HUMAN RESOURCES

The organisation of control — at head office level — differs from one country to another, first because of the different nature of the organisation structures; and second because the functions of the control departments are not equivalent. In Great Britain, the main function is to participate in the elaboration of budgets, accounting procedures and reporting systems, and to collect performance measurements and look at or highlight major deviations. In addition control departments will deal with long-range planning (e.g., setting procedures and probing plans) when it is not done by a separate department: that is for five out of thirteen which have long-range plans. In Germany, the controller's function follows two quite different patterns. In some cases, the control department deals with accounting, cost accounting and/or auditing and data processing. In the other pattern, a single person — or two to five persons — will deal with planning (both long-term and short-term) and monitoring performance against plan, whereas cost accounting, accounting and EDP are separated.

In France, budgetary control for more sophisticated firms is separated from accounting and finance, and looks more like the second model of German organisation. For the latter two countries, however, control and accounting are intermingled.

TABLE 6.2 Organisation of central control department by main tasks

	Great Britain	Germany	France
Budget and control only	15	4	4
Budget, control and cost accounting[a]	0	7	6
Budget, control and EDP	1	2	0
Budget, control, EDP and cost accounting	0	4	2

[a] Mainly in these two cases, the department will additionally carry long-range planning tasks.

$p < .05$.

They will have to be treated as such. Table 6.2 summarises the main functions of the head office control departments.

IN GREAT BRITAIN: A HEAVY DOTTED LINE

Most British firms have a central financial control department at headquarters with about two to six people in it. Its main tasks are to set up the budgetary process; design management control formats especially for top management reporting; help subsidiaries with procedures; aggregate their results and highlight major deviations; and finally participate in performance review sessions.

Each subsidiary product-market unit and/or division will have its own financial director or financial controller or chief accountant who – besides his accounting and/or cost-accounting role – will elaborate, devise and run the management control system necessary for the unit managing director. He will be, as many central financial controllers said, linked by a 'heavy dotted line' to the central financial controller.

IN GERMANY: MOVE FROM *KONTROLLE* TO CONTROLLING

In the German firms studied, and probably in German firms as a group, there seems to have been an evolution with respect to control which is reflected in the different control departments

Top Management—The Controllership Function 109

and functions seen. It is possible to distinguish two extreme philosophies of control.

The first one relies heavily on past performance, accounting or cost-accounting data and information; reporting is mostly done on costs and efficiency, following fiscal accounting rules and formats. It gives top management essentially output, personnel, gross margin and all costs attributed to particular products and/or units of the firm. The information does not, except for costs, delineate the responsibility and accountability of particular departments. The variances, whenever calculated, serve mostly to see whether the level of activity and performance is acceptable and whether the company as a whole is making money or not. Cost accounting is dominant in order to allow for the calculation of product profit contribution and production units' efficiency. Those firms which have gone away from this philosophy call it *Kontrolle* (or accounting — *Rechnungswesen*).

This approach based on the past (ex-post control), providing very detailed information up to the top, has been widely criticised; an example is provided by several articles written by a partner of McKinsey Germany[1] and summarised in the following excerpt:

> As a central monitoring and control instrument, as practiced in Germany, cost accounting can be criticised as not being precise, not up to date, not economically orientated, failing to provide some means of comparisons, not understanding as well as not being able to comprehend the most interesting costs.

At the other extreme, a new function and position has been created, using an American word for it — 'controlling', as illustrated by the following description of a position.[2] (see figure 6.1.)

In this approach, the functions of the controller are much broader, as indicated on the following abridged job description of one of the controllers interviewed.

> In German the word which describes the role of the American controller (to control) will be often too quickly linked with the word *Kontrolle*, which is the direct translation, but

Unsere weltweit operierende Gruppe ist in weitgehend selbständige, jeweils ergebnisverantwortliche Unternehmenseinheiten gegliedert. Mit Hilfe der Zentralbereiche steuern wir das Unternehmen. Dazu gehört auch das

Controlling

Für diesen Zentralbereich suchen wir einen Mitarbeiter mit abgeschlossener Hochschulbildung für folgende Aufgaben:

— Aufstellung von Plan- und Budgetrichtlinien
— Unterstützung und Beratung der Geschäftsbereiche
— permanente Kostenkontrolle und Analyse von Abweichungen
— Investitions- und Risikoanalysen
— Mitwirkung im Rahmen der laufenden Berichterstattung

Unser neuer Mitarbeiter sollte bereits Erfahrung gesammelt haben im Controlling international orientierter Unternehmen — vorzugsweise im Maschinenbau —, über Kenntnisse des betrieblichen Rechnungswesens, einschließlich Grenzkostenrechnung, verfügen und mit Einsatz und Anwendung der EDV vertraut sein. Französische Sprachkenntnisse sind erwünscht.

Herren bis Mitte 30 mit analytischer Denkweise und praxisorientiert, die befähigt sind, diese interessante Aufgabe zu übernehmen, bitten wir um ihre Bewerbungsunterlagen mit Angabe des frühesten Eintrittstermines und Gehaltsvorstellung an

FIG. 6.1 Controlling required

instead we should use the word '*steuern*' (to guide). In this short word lies the function of the controller — that is to guide and regulate the different activities of a firm with a plan so that the defined objectives of the firm may be achieved. In our firm in the beginning of 1976 a new service

Top Management—The Controllership Function 111

'*Zentralles Controlling*' has been created, dependent on the finance *Vorstand*. Out of the global definition just given, the main tasks of the Central Controlling are:

— formulation and establishment of the basis of planning and budgeting for the group;
— permanent plan-performance comparisons;
— analysis and interpretation of variances as well as assistance of departments in the elaboration of corrective action plans;
— continuous reporting on relevant information to management, outside financial matters;
— assistance to central finance and accounting especially in management accounting principles;
— economic analyses.

Many firms investigated try to get away from the *Kontrolle* approach and move towards the 'controlling' side, involving much more long-term and short-term planning, objective-setting, evaluation of performance, reporting of large variances and initiating of corrective actions. The word *Kontrolle* has a connotation of surveillance that people do not want to use. In terms of function and organisation, the consequences of such different approaches are two-fold. First, in *Kontrolle* the controller is likely to be dealing mostly with accounting, cost accounting and the calculus of standard costing. He is likely to have either a rather large staff or correspondents at the factory level, and also to be the head of the data-processing department and/or audit or fiscal accounting. At the other extreme, the controlling man will be separated from cost accounting, standard costing and accounting, EDP and organisation, although he will still usually be under the same superior (finance and administration *Vorstand*). He is likely to have only a small staff of his own. As one chief executive of an 11,000-employee firm said: 'To move to a real top management planning and control system it has required us only to add two and a half men to our organisation.'

Some firms have also put such a man at each divisional level; others, organised by functions, have assigned such a man to each function (e.g., marketing 'controlling' and production 'controlling').

There are some people in Germany[3] who even argue that instead of having functional specialists at the *Vorstand* level, one should consider more generalists, one of which would be the 'controlling' chief executive.

Which factors will make a firm lean towards one of the two extremes? The researcher's impression is that size may play a certain role (smaller firms leaning more towards simple cost accounting and *Kontrolle*); this corresponds also to more centralisation of decision-making. But more important, perhaps, is the introduction of outside management when the company becomes public or less dominated by family or 'founder' management: a more modern approach than simple cost control usually follows. Finally, divisional organisations are more likely to lean towards 'controlling' than their functional counterparts.

THE CONTROLLER IN FRANCE: TWO ROLES

The impression in France is that the controller (*Le Contrôleur de Gestion*) is either young and bright (but his boss does not always follow him) or he comes from engineering and likes good analytical exhaustive management-information systems.

The French controller is usually separated from the finance department and accounting department. In most instances he reports directly to the chief executive. He may have a central staff which deals with a particular side of the business (sales controller, production controller).

In some cases he may have a business education, be rather young and have budgetary control as his chief function. He may be over-eager to act as a consultant to the chief executive and to line personnel but, in fact, does not really participate in setting objectives.

In other cases, in fact, his role is confined to one which is similar to the *Kontrolle*-type seen in Germany, with a heavy emphasis on fiscal and cost accounting. Surprisingly, he will often come from engineering: in this case, he is likely to look for heavy, computer-based, exhaustive information systems.

SOME ELEMENTS OF CONTROL COSTS

The structure of control described above, according to the three countries, gives the average number of people working on

Top Management—The Controllership Function

TABLE 6.3 Average number of people working in management control, at headquarters in the marketing, production and finance domains

	Great Britain	Germany	France
Total	35·8	27·7	24·6
Headquarters	5·1	7·8	8·1
Marketing	·5	2·2	1·3
Production	·0	9·3	12·4
Finance	2·3	1·7	0·6
Other[a]	30·0	6·7	2·2

[a] These are mainly controllers situated at subsidiary or divisional levels.

control (accounting and cost-accounting personnel were eliminated to focus on management control) (Table 6.3).

These figures require some comment. On its face value — size of firms being equal — Table 6.3 would suggest that control requires more people in Great Britain than in Germany and France and thus costs more. This is not the case, because computers are not used in Great Britain for control purposes whereas they are in France and Germany. Besides, the information system is very much integrated in these latter two countries, which means that both computer and personnel costs may be under-emphasised as cost-accounting people are an important ingredient of control; computer runs and costs for control purposes have often been described as by-products of a quite exhaustive data basis for invoicing, inventory control, fiscal accounting, cost accounting, buying, etc., which means only that 5–20 per cent of computer costs was covered by the estimated costs of pure financial control. Three out of fifteen British firms for which data were made available use computers and the cost was estimated between $16,000 and $80,000 per year. Seven out of ten French firms for which data were available mentioned using the computer and the cost varies between $40,000 and $200,000. Eleven out of fourteen German firms for which data were available use computers and the cost varies between $400,000 and $860,000.

For some French and German firms, in which the total cost of computer use was given (e.g., financial control and also cost accounting) the computer cost has to be multiplied by between five and ten and the number of people by three.

As evidence of the close link of accounting with management control in France and Germany only became clear during the research, data were not available on the number of people working in cost accounting for all firms. Altogether, then, the issue of cost control is difficult to settle in this study.

THE DATA BASE: COST AND PROFIT ACCOUNTING: EMPHASIS ON REPORTING TO TOP MANAGEMENT

The design of the information system upon which top management control is exercised is in some respects the result of cost accounting and profit-centre accounting, at least for the financial aspect of control. Other information dealing with output, deliveries, sales, orders, personnel, machine and plant loading, capital expenditure, cash flow, source and disposition of funds and elements of working capital also provide a basis for control. Such elements as were described in the previous chapter account for the level of activity and cash proceedings. They cannot be used as a base for the monitoring of profit performance. Cost and profit accounting can aid many decisions and lead to several corrective actions — such as pricing decisions, the decision on optimal product mix, make or buy decisions, resource allocation among units, evaluation of management and bonus schemes, reduction of costs and abandonment of certain products.

With respect to cost and profit accounting, major differences were found between the three countries, which in turn account for major differences in the way the control documents are presented to top management.

Roughly speaking, at one extreme British firms make little use of cost accounting at central office level, and are mainly interested in overall profit results. At the other extreme — still from the head office point of view — in Germany, cost and profit accounting is dealt with in a very detailed fashion and reported to top management. French firms are in between, leaning much towards the German system with less standardisation and systematisation.

It does not mean, however, that British firms do not use cost accounting but that information and the resulting decisions are left to the decentralised units. In France and Germany, central staff centralise, work out, compute and monitor costs.

Some German firms have even split the cost-accounting department into two: one department deals with production, sales or divisional unit costs and profit accounting; the other with headquarters administration cost accounting. In one company, for instance, the controller reported that there were forty centres for a total headquarters staff of 150 people! How costs and profits arrive at the control department determine in large part what information will be supplied to top management.

COST ACCOUNTING AND COST CENTRES

Cost accounting has been found to be in use for about twenty-five years in Great Britain and Germany, and for about fourteen years in France, on the average. There are marked differences in the size of the unit which serves as a cost centre, as Table 6.4 below indicates.

There is some variation according to the sector, principally for those firms in electronics and mechanical engineering who do not work on standard equipment but on tailor-made, unique, heavy equipment. But, by and large, as may be seen in the first line of Table 6.4, in Germany and France the smallest frequently used cost unit is the workshop.

TABLE 6.4   Which units serve as bases for cost centres?

Cost-centre unit	Great Britain[a]	Germany[a]	France[a]
	%	%	%
Workshop	25	82	72
Part of plant	50	70	55
Plant	42	70	63
Product	42	94	73
Administration	58	88	91
Other[b]	50	35	53

[a] Based on twelve observations for Great Britain, seventeen in Germany and eleven in France.

[b] Such as whole production unit or regional sales office, etc.

Although costs are fairly detailed to the smallest unit in Germany and France, it does not always mean that the standards against which performance will be measured are based on planning: many of those standards will be based on last year's costs more than on the analysis of alternative courses of action as illustrated in Table 6.5.

TABLE 6.5 Average proportion in the basis for establishing cost centre's objectives

	Great Britain	Germany	France
	%	%	%
Last year's result	21	**61**	**47**
Short-range (one year) planning	29	24	29
Long-range planning	**50**	15	24
Total	100	100	100

In fact, the association between detailed tiny unit cost accounting and standards based on the past may be a causal one.

Although this table does not take into account, especially for Germany, the presence of two control extremes, it shows a heavier emphasis on the past which corroborates a conservative, past-oriented – not so strategic – approach found in several German and many French firms.

'PROFIT ACCOUNTING' AND PROFIT CENTRES

Because of the difference in management structure in the three countries, one must distinguish profit accounting and profit centres.

Profit accounting is a means by which some sort of profit contribution will be calculated by product and/or market, although there is not one man or team responsible for that product uniquely. It serves as a basis for pricing decisions, product mix decisions, resource allocation, etc.

On the other hand, profit centres refer to the responsibility a manager has over the profit of his activity. It is usually the case in divisional or product-market subsidiary type of structure. It can also be the case in functional organisations, when either sales or production, or both, are treated as profit centres and transfer prices installed between them.

The main difference which appears between countries is the accumulation of both the profit accounting and profit centres types of reporting systems in the German, the precedence of profit accounting in the French information system, whereas British accounting is mainly in terms of profit centres, as shown in Table 6.6.

TABLE 6.6 Basis of profit accounting

	Great Britain[a]	Germany[a]	France[a]
	%	%	%
Part of plant	12	7	0
Plant	6	21	36
Product	23	78	54
Market	6	50	27
Division	41	57	18
Other[b]	**100**	50	36

[a] Based on respectively seventeen British, fourteen German and twelve French observations.
[b] Mainly product market subsidiaries.

This table suggests the following characterisations of practice in each country.

In the British system, each subsidiary will be considered as a profit centre by top management; sometimes the 'division' as described in Chapter 4 (e.g. with a divisional chairman or chief executive), will also be considered as a profit centre. Products as profit centre will only arise for functional firms and/or for firms working on large unique tailor-made products.

On the other hand, the German companies have both types of profit recording: the one which is under the responsibility of

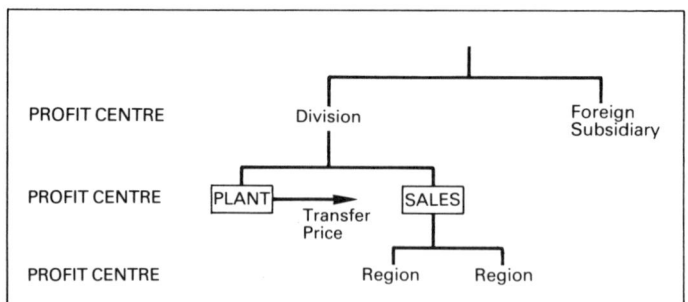

FIG. 6.2 Profit centre accountability: division, sales and production departments in the German company

a manager, and the one which serves as an information basis (see figures 6.2 and 6.3).

In the companies seen, there may be as many as 10,000 products for which such profit accounting is done or as many as one hundred to five hundred product (*Kostentrager*) groups.

In French firms, at least sophisticated ones – i.e., with a structure including several production units specialised by product and several sales units specialised by markets or products – the production unit will be treated as a profit centre (its objective being zero profit) and the sales units will also be treated as profit centres. Thus, both production and sales variances will be analysed.

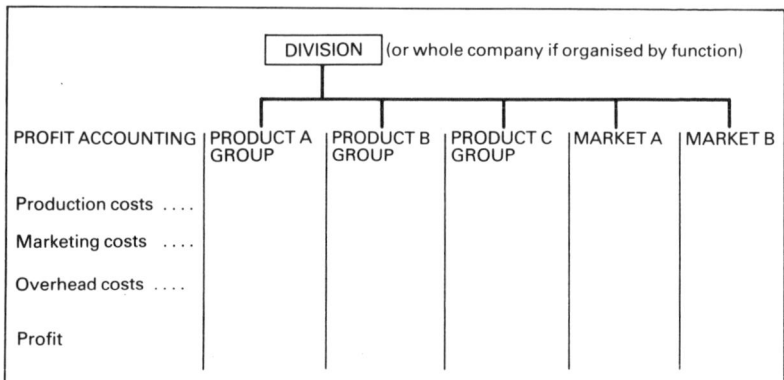

FIG. 6.3 Profit accounting: product and/or market in the German company

The profit-centre system (not the profit-accounting one) is much younger in Germany (six years) and in France (nine years) than in Great Britain (seventeen years) which attests to a late evolution from simple profit accounting to profit accountability.

For a particular unit there are at least two possibilities for reporting sales: in model S_1, used in most British companies, only one sales figure per unit is provided, whereas in model S_2, sales figures are given per product line and/or product group to top management.

For a particular unit, variable costs may be reported for the whole unit (V_1) but they may also be broken down into several items (manufacturing, selling), reported on a per product basis (V_2) which always, in this case, leads to reporting different costs items per product. (In Great Britain the number of items may run up to three or four; in Germany and on a per product basis, individual items may be as high as fifteen.)

Finally, fixed costs may be reported for the whole unit, as one item (F_1) or through several items (F_2) (wages, transport, electricity, etc.) or per product, or applying full costing (F_3) to each product, allocating to the products some fixed costs and imputing others to the unit as a whole (F_4).

As this figure 6.4 shows, most British firms will *not* single out individual products when reporting to top management. Rather, the overall sales, variable costs and fixed costs are emphasised. It corroborates the fact that decisions and initiatives on corrective actions rely heavily on the subsidiaries to achieve general sales and profit goals: detailed costs are not specified. On the other end of the spectrum, coherent with the low degree of delegation found, most German firms have a report to top management done by product group for each unit. This in turn means that product profits are calculated by single product lines down the line — for instance, whereas six product groups per division are reported to top management, costs may have been imputed to two hundred products by cost accounting.

As a second difference, documents show that most of the costs are reported following fiscal accounting procedures and accounts — e.g., instead of having variable selling costs, one would have wages, transport, etc., which are account headings similar to fiscal accounting and ledger accounts. As a third difference, and as a result of reporting by product, many

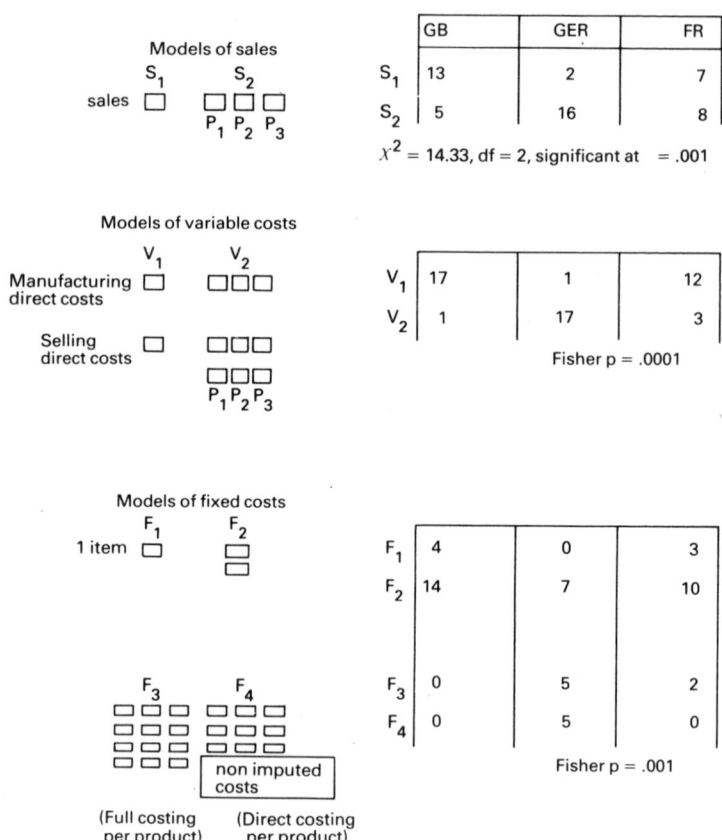

FIG. 6.4 Reporting system design

companies use full costing for *products* with imputed headquarters and overhead costs (model F_3). Finally, parallel to it and often computed centrally, all cost centres' performances will also be available, although they do not usually go to top management, being analysed instead by the control department.

In France, only nine out of sixteen firms produce unit income statements with sales and costs put together. For the others, sales and sales administration budgets, when they exist, are not divided by months. As a result profit control is available only in so far as production costs are budgeted per month, thus making production profit control possible: the factory is a profit centre more often than a product-market unit.

The above-mentioned differences lead one to think that central staff and top management are much more involved in the detailed profit control of units in Germany and France than in Great Britain. However, as many of these profit performance reports follow fiscal accounting rules more than managerial accounting principles, one may wonder about the possible corrective steps that may be taken, either by unit or by product group! Significant in this respect is the fact that whereas 82 per cent of British firms use return on investment to evaluate a unit performance, only 31 per cent do so in Germany and 27 per cent in France.

SHORT-RANGE PLANNING AND CONTROL

It seems to be well ingrained in most firms investigated that some sort of one-year planning and control has to be made. There are, however, different degrees to which those one-year plans are designed and worked out. Profit planning and control, just described above, shows a different degree of detail in the three countries. Budgets and/or one-year plans can deal with revenues (sales), costs (both variables and fixed, production and marketing, administration and R & D), with financing (source and disposition of funds, cash budget) and with capital expenditure.

Whereas some sort of budgeting is done in all three countries it has not been done for as long in Germany and France as in Great Britain.

The researcher's impression is that if firms just under the size of the ones chosen had been investigated in France, and to a lesser degree in Germany, one would not have found budgets

TABLE 6.7 Number of years companies have had budgets

Great Britain	Germany	France
15 years	8 years	8 years

yet, although these firms would still have been in the top five hundred in their country.

Two budget features seem to differentiate the firms by country.

CONTENT AND CYCLE

The documents provided by chief executives and controllers show that in Great Britain most aspects of the activity are budgeted by unit. The managing director will propose sales, profit, source and disposition of funds, cash flow, cash and capital expenditure budgets as part of the planning process after long-range plans have been discussed and approved. They will represent a firm commitment for next year (see figure 6.5).

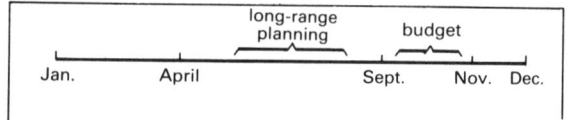

FIG. 6.5 The British planning cycle

German firms emphasise financing and cash budgeting for units much less. This is mostly a result of the structure, as cash proceedings are centralised. Also, financing and liquidity do not seem to be a major problem in Germany (because of low interest rates). In 1977, a source indicates that altogether German firms have used only 30 per cent of their banking facilities. Whereas financing is less emphasised, costs budgets are on the contrary more emphasised, whether they deal with production or sales or whether they deal with administration. In addition, and as part of the one-year planning, extensive definition of objectives is required from managers in those aspects of the business they direct. Lists of tasks, potential dates of completion and results are required. This aspect may be reinforced in companies using the 'controlling' philosophy described earlier where the same man is in charge of planning and controlling. The emphasis on one-year planning is so important that often the budget proposed

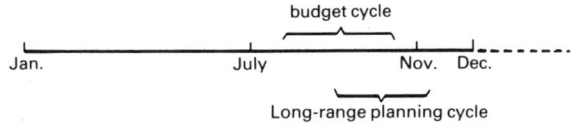

FIG. 6.6 The German planning cycle

and discussed by managers is completed before the long-range plans (see figure 6.6).

Whereas one can say that fifteen out of the sixteen French firms studied have some overall sales/expenses budgets for the year, monthly profit budgets (sales expenses) are present in only nine firms, whereas monthly production budgets exist for fourteen out of sixteen. Capital expenditure seems to be quite often a domain reserved to top management, as well as financing and cash.

THE INFLUENCE OF THE CONTROLLER

The influence of the controller in the budgetary control also varies by country. Whereas reports on budget performance in Great Britain are in most cases prepared by the unit, it is not always so in France and Germany (see Table 6.8).

TABLE 6.8 Who prepares reports on budget results?

	Great Britain	Germany	France
Controller	6	15	11
Units	10	2	1

Fisher p = ·0028

For France and Germany, it is therefore not surprising to see on those budget results, notes written by the control department.

Table 6.9 reveals a somewhat higher influence of staff on operations and a more active 'watchdog' approach.

TABLE 6.9 Controller's input on budget results sent to unit

	Great Britain	Germany	France
Has recommendations or orders, or requests for supplementary information	3	9	5
Does not	15	9	10

$\chi^2 = 3.36$, df = 1, $\alpha = .10$

SUMMARY

The opinions of central controllers concerning the objectives of control resemble those chief executive officers and thus confirm the national differences described in the previous chapter. The exception to this pattern in which British controllers stress strict adherence to control procedures more heavily than their superiors, may also be explained in terms of national differences in organisational structure: British controllers are better placed to see that close attention to procedure is fundamental in a holding company to ensure at least a minimum of compatibility and standardisation in the way information is supplied to top managers. As to the influence of the central controller in overall control, one may be led to think that French and German controllers are much more involved in operational matters than their British counterparts. This view is confirmed by the higher degree of centralisation in the gathering of information on performance, the much more detailed inflow of operational information on product profit and department costs for each unit to central offices in Germany and to a lesser degree in France. It is also revealed by the higher degree of detail required in setting short-range objectives in Germany as well as by the annotations or initiatives taken there by the controller (recommendations, requests for additional information, etc.).

Profit-control reporting to top management has been stressed, as it revealed to the researcher a striking difference between countries: Germany and France differ strongly from Great Britain in this respect.

Cost accounting and general accounting have a larger influence in Germany and France, resulting in reports useful for fiscal accounting and consolidation purposes but less so for management control.

All these aspects seem to be quite coherent with the differential emphasis in planning and degree of delegation.

The next chapter closes the description of differences and similarities by looking at production and marketing control.

NOTES

1. Herbert Henzler, 'Angriff auf ein Tabu', Art., n.p., (April 1975); see also 'Der Januskopf muss weg!', *Wirtschaftwoche*, vol. 38 (13 September 1974).
2. *Die Frankfurter Allgemeine Zeitung*, n.d.
3. F. Hoffmann, 'Der Controller in Deutschen Industriebetrieb', *Der Betrieb*, vol. 21 (December 1968) pp. 2181, 2185.

7 Operational Control: Marketing and Production

SCOPE OF CHAPTER

This chapter covers the application of the control philosophies and system designs described previously in two functional areas of the firm: marketing and production. The emphasis is on country differences and similarities with respect to the degree of formalism in control systems and to the 'tightness' of the control process: what standards are set and by whom; how performance is measured, at what frequency and by whom; what is reported and who evaluates performance. Marketing and production, selected as the two main operational areas of the firm, were found to be differentially emphasised by chief executives and controllers. Therefore, in order to deepen and sharpen our understanding of management control we analyse how line managers in both areas envision the monitoring of performance. Finally, we compare the marketing and production viewpoints in order to assess the differences between these two areas with respect to the use of control.

THE BASIC OBJECTIVES PURSUED IN OPERATIONAL CONTROL

No overall difference was found between answers of marketing and production managers within each country as to which objectives are pursued in control. (A Chi square test was performed between marketing and production executives on each of the twelve questions concerning control objectives within each country. No significant differences appeared.) Besides, most marketing and production managers agree with their bosses. (A Mann Whitney U test, similar to the one performed between chief executives and controllers, was used to compare chief executives on one side vs managers (marketing and production) on the other side according to the three factors composing control objectives. (U = 120, n.s.) This reinforces the idea of differences between countries already expressed in Chapters 5 and 6 and intra-country homogeneity with respect to control objectives. However, when looking closely at the data (i.e., individual questions composing these factors), there are two significant intra-country differences, but these too can best be explained in terms of national differences.

Whereas British chief executives do not view the policing instrument uses of control as a major objective, data suggest a different viewpoint is held by both marketing and production managers. This may be a result of the particular management style in Britain: in fact, marketing and production managers are much closer to operations than their boss. They usually belong to small units where their role is more to see that orders and procedures are carried out, as defined, by subordinates — a task that group executives cannot perform within the prevailing decentralised basic structure and philosophy.

Thus, statistically significant differences were identified (Tables 7.1 and 7.2) with respect to two aspects of control: to ensure that (a) procedures and (b) orders are carried out as defined.

These figures suggest a changing focus of control when one gets nearer operations in Great Britain: it turns from a guiding instrument into more of a policing instrument. It should be noted that the latter emphasis was frequently observed at chief

TABLE 7.1 Control ensures that *procedures* are carried out, as defined, by subordinates

	Chief executives	Line managers
Agree or strongly agree	8	17
Disagree	9	4

Fisher p = ·012.

TABLE 7.2 Control ensures that *orders* are carried out, as defined, by subordinates

	Chief executives	Line managers
Agree or strongly agree	4	14
Disagree	11	7

Fisher p = ·02.

executive levels in France and Germany. This was due to the fact that, in these countries, chief executives are closer to operations than their British counterparts, which is exemplified by the higher frequency and degree of detail with which their control instruments are designed (profit by product, daily orders or sales) and presumably used — or at least watched — by them. In Great Britain, profit planning and control, which was seen in extremely general terms at the group level, becomes much more detailed at subsidiary level.

The other significant intra-country difference appears in France where operational managers do not appear to think that one of the main purposes of control is to keep the boss informed, or at least they think so less than their bosses (Table 7.3).

After setting up a subsidiary in France, the chief executive of a large British firm was assailed by his French executives. They were complaining that power was too concentrated at headquarters. Intrigued by the criticism, he asked British and French managers what types of decisions should be decentralised at

TABLE 7.3 Control's objective is to keep the boss informed of what is going on in the organisation

	Chief executives	Line managers
Strongly agree or agree	13	7
Disagree	1	10

Fisher p = ·003

Operational Control: Marketing and Production 129

their level and also what types of decisions they were themselves prepared to decentralise down the line. His report:

> I was struck by the difference. The French wanted everything for themselves but did not want to share any part of it with their subordinates, whereas British managers were prepared to go both ways.

This example, along with Table 7.3, may suggest a French cultural bias: everybody wants autonomy for himself but not for the others, and especially not for his subordinates.

THE ESSENTIAL CHARACTERISTICS OF CONTROL AND THE RESULTING DEGREE OF FORMALISM IN OPERATIONS CONTROL

Overall, production control is more formal than marketing control in the three countries investigated. By more formal, we mean a higher frequency of control and checking on subordinates' decisions, a more comprehensive use of rules for control and of specific quantitative criteria in order to evaluate departmental and individual performances (figure 7.1)

This formalism varies, however, within each country and between countries. On a per-country basis there is a marked difference between marketing and production managers in Germany and Great Britain but not in France (figure 7.2).

Comparing production control across countries (see figure 7.3), we find that it is more formal in Germany and less so in France, with Great Britain lying in between. In so far as market-

Mann Whitney $Z = 1.74$, $\alpha = .04$

FIG. 7.1 Interfunction comparative degree of formalism in operational control

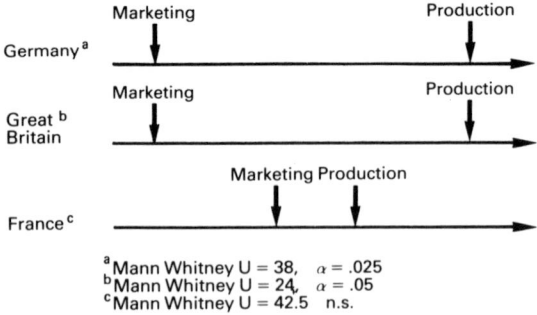

FIG. 7.2 Intra-country differential degree of formalism in operational control

ing control is concerned, there are only slight differences in formalism across countries.

A closer look at country-by-country differences in the components which make up control formalism (shown in Table 7.4) sheds more light on the reasons for these differences. The table summarises in a verbal format differences seen in the quantitative measurements and substantiated by managers' comments.

Thus, in the case of Germany, the higher degree of formalism in production as compared to marketing is due much more to the use of more specific criteria for the evaluation of individual and departmental performance and to closer supervision than to the use of more comprehensive rules. In Great Britain, a reversed set of emphases accounts for the higher formalism in production. In France, the generally similar degree of formalism in production and marketing is reached through the influence of off-setting emphases. On the one hand production control is more frequent and rules are more comprehensive in production

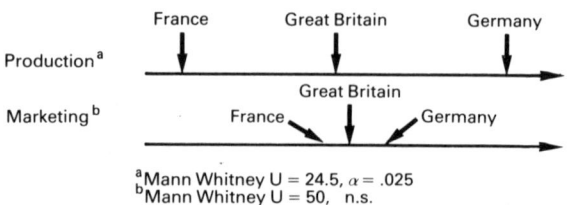

FIG. 7.3 Inter-country differential degree of formalism in operational control

TABLE 7.4 Characteristics of operational control in each country

	Marketing	Production
Germany		
Frequency		Similar
Use of rules		Similar
Check on subordinates' decisions	Looser	Tighter
Criteria for evaluation of performance	Less specific	More specific
Link of control with rewards	Looser	Tighter
Great Britain		
Frequency	Lower	Higher
Use of rules	Lower	Higher
Check on subordinates' decisions		Similar
Criteria for evaluation of performance		Similar
Link of control with rewards		Similar
France		
Frequency	Lower	Higher
Use of rules	Lower	Higher
Check on subordinates' decisions	Tighter	Looser
Criteria for evaluation of performance		Similar
Link of control with rewards	Tighter	Looser

than in marketing. On the other hand, there is a closer link between results and evaluation of managers as well as a closer supervision in marketing than in production.

Table 7.4 would suggest that German managers, whatever their functions, are very systematic in setting rules of behaviour and, like their chief executives, want to check on things frequently, although the kinds of tasks to be performed may not be similar. In production, which they strongly emphasised (as described above), they supervise matters closely, congruent with the lower degree of decentralisation found in that country. The

British, on the other hand — when dealing with the more short-term quantitative problems that may be found in production — seem to prefer to increase rules and the frequency of control rather than to depart from the spirit of delegation by supervising more closely as in the German case.

Turning to the between-country differences in production control (i.e., significantly higher formalism in Germany than in France) we find that the closeness of supervision as well as the specificity with which criteria are set in Germany account for the differences with France.

The above data would suggest that production control, which seems to be a strength — or at least emphasised everywhere — in German management, requires not only that rules be comprehensive and control frequency high but also that supervision be quite close, specific criteria be set and links provided with rewards. French and British managers do not seem to enforce these last three requirements as much as the Germans. As a possible explanation, one could venture that discipline is higher in German companies, enabling them to use close supervision. An alternative explanation stresses the closer link found with rewards in Germany, where many production managers emphasised that they were obliged by unions to be quite specific on the individual rating system used to promote or reward the workers according to their achievements. Whereas often no formal evaluation of performance — such as an annual appraisal — was in effect for general managers or marketing managers, appraisal forms with elaborate rating systems, imposed by unions and the workers' participation in the 'board of directors', were most of the time present for production workers. (In Germany, the *Aufsichtsrat* (council of surveillance) is composed of one third workers; the proportion is soon to be increased to one half.)

'TIGHTNESS OF GRASP': A COMPARATIVE VIEW OF THE CONTROL PROCESS

By tighter grasp we mean a way of defining standards against which performance is to be evaluated as well as ways of measuring this performance frequently enough not only for objectives —

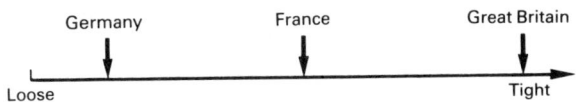

FIG. 7.4 Degree of grasp in marketing

which are easy to set pars for — and measures but also for more qualitative objectives.

Cross-country comparisons essentially indicate, with respect to the marketing control process, that British marketing managers have a relatively tight grasp on marketing.

French managers are middle of the road and German managers lie on the looser side (see figure 7.4).

In production, an opposite ranking is observed: German managers have a tighter grasp than French or British managers in the order indicated in figure 7.5.

Those two figures give only the tendencies, although, once again, they are not at all meant to represent any sort of scaling. They summarise and aggregate several indications of this 'grasp' in operational control which are detailed below, first in marketing, then in production.

THE MARKETING CONTROL PROCESS: STANDARD SETTING, MEASUREMENT AND EVALUATION OF PERFORMANCE

Each marketing manager was asked to choose the five most important objectives among those which are commonly assigned to marketing. The suggested list included 28 objectives, of which 13 were 'quantitative operational' and 15 'qualitative non-operational'.

A 'quantitative operational', objective is one which can directly be transformed into a quantitative norm or standard against which to measure performance. An example is sales

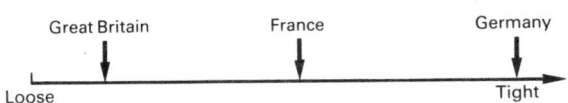

FIG. 7.5 Degree of grasp in production

growth, which can be translated into a straight standard of X per cent growth for next year; other such objectives include market share and product profit contribution.

'Qualitative non-operational' objectives are not directly translatable into quantitative standards. One must set indirect indicators and a par for each indicator if one wants to define standards. Performance can then be measured against those pars. Such objectives included image, quality, customer loyalty, coordination with production or supervision of sales force. In such objectives, if no standard is set, but if a measure is available, the basis for action will usually involve comparing this year's performance with last year's performance. If no measure is available, only the subjective managerial opinion is available to make an evaluation and take corrective action. For instance, customer loyalty may be such an objective. With no standards set but performance being measured by the number of customers who have left the company over a fixed period, or by the number of repeat orders from a particular customer, one can compare two measurements between two points in time. As another example, one may set image building as an objective: if neither indicators nor measures of performance are selected, only the manager's subjective evaluation will serve as a basis for corrective action.

It appears that British marketing managers have such a firm grasp of their activity because of the higher degree with which they have been able to specify indicators or standards as well as measures for qualitative non-operational objectives, as we shall see in what follows.

The number of times operational and non-operational marketing objectives were listed as being part of the five most important control objectives of the firm are given in Table 7.5. Only those cases for which a complete data set on the entire control process was available were considered; 21 incomplete observations were eliminated.

Noting that for an operational objective a standard and a measure are always present, Table 7.6 below indicates, for non-operational marketing objectives only, the number of times a quantitative standard was given, as well as the number of times when a measure was present (with or without standard given).

One could explain this difference by the types of non-operational objectives chosen in Great Britain as against those chosen

TABLE 7.5 Number of times operational and non-operational marketing objectives have been selected in the top five by marketing managers

	Great Britain	Germany	France
Qualitative non-operational	23	19	10
Quantitative operational	23	19	13
Total	46	38	23

in France or Germany. However, there is no evidence that British managers select objectives which are concentrated in any particular area, or that their goals are different from their German or French counterparts. In fact, British managers, in choosing five top goals from the list of 28 marketing objectives in the interview guideline, tapped the most diverse set of objectives: altogether the ten or so British marketing managers selected as the five most important ones 22 objectives out of a possible list of 29. The same goes for Germany (16) and for France (18).

As nearly the whole spectrum of possible marketing objectives was selected, with no particular concentration in any subgroup of objectives, one may deduce that British managers seem to be

TABLE 7.6 The treatment of non-operational marketing objectives in control

	Great Britain	Germany	France
Have standards[a] and are measured	11	5	3
Have *no* standards but are measured	6	3	5
Have *no* standards[b] and are *not* measured	6	11	2
	23	19	10

[a] $\chi^2 = 2\cdot 38$, df = 1, $\alpha = \cdot 10$ (Great Britain vs block of France and Germany)
[b] $\chi^2 = 6$, df = 2, $\alpha = \cdot 05$

better equipped to handle marketing factors than their German counterparts. This is congruent with their higher emphasis on the longer term and with their better handling of qualitative data that was already present at top management level.

As a consequence of this tighter grasp in standard setting and performance measurement in Great Britain, the time span between checks on performance is shorter (see Table 7.7).

TABLE 7.7 Time span of marketing performance measurement

	Great Britain		Germany		France	
A month or less	82%	32	69%	22	73%	22
Above a month	18%	7	31%	10	27%	8

It is much simpler and more useful to measure performance more often when specific standards have been set up than in their absence. For instance, in a French mechanical engineering firm the marketing manager mentioned image as one of the five most important objectives. No specific standards with pars were set up. Top management simply said that all communications with the outside should be 'good', especially with customers. To measure performance, he had his secretary take samples of letters going out to customers only. Once a year he could make a report to top management on the way he felt communications with customers had been treated, and usually which corrective action was needed. This resulted in memos on how to improve letter-writing and presentation, based on his subjective evaluation, being sent to the different departments.

These data would seem to indicate a difficulty among German marketing managers in defining quantitative par values for non-operational marketing objectives. Additional data tend to indicate that this might be the result of a higher influence of headquarters in marketing control in German companies.

Whereas marketing managers indicate that the standards are set by the chief executive in only 46 per cent of cases in Great Britain and 30 per cent of cases in France, German marketing managers indicate that this is so in 76 per cent of their cases. They also indicate that in 62 per cent of the cases measurement is done outside of their department, where this is only true for

Operational Control: Marketing and Production

TABLE 7.8 Who defines marketing standards?

	Great Britain	Germany	France
	%	%	%
The marketing department or the controller	54	24	70
The chief executive	46	76	30
Total	100	100	100

37 and 33 per cent of cases in France and Great Britain (see Table 7.8).

In addition, to arrive at this tighter standard setting and performance measurement, British and French managers are likely to get more complete reports, including material on positive as well as negative deviations, whereas German managers use exception principles more.

Finally although the evaluation is often made by top management in all three countries, one must notice that whereas in France and Great Britain *no* marketing managers indicated that evaluation could be done by the controller, German marketing managers said it happened in 21 per cent of cases. The intrusion of controllers, i.e. staff, in evaluation, may lead to a loss of control by the line in non-operational matters where the controllers are not very interested or skilled enough to define proper standards.

The presentation of the marketing control process seems to indicate that part of the reason why German marketing control is not so tight may stem from the higher influence of headquarters both in standard setting, in measurement and evaluation.

TABLE 7.9 Who measures marketing performance?

	Great Britain	Germany	France
	%	%	%
The marketing department	63	37	67
The controller or chief executive	37	63	33
Total	100	100	100

TABLE 7.10 What is included in reports?

	Great Britain	Germany	France
	%	%	%
Everything	80	50	88
Exceptions, or only positive, or only negative deviations	20	50	12
Total	100	100	100

By over-centralising and thus not allowing self control, it becomes more difficult to define proper indicators and pars for some objectives which, although they are qualitative, are still very important. As the degree of formalism in marketing in Germany is low, specific criteria for performance evaluation are lacking and thus control is looser. On the other side, more self control seems to be associated with tighter operational marketing control — as in the British case.

THE PRODUCTION CONTROL PROCESS: STANDARD SETTING, MEASUREMENT OF PERFORMANCE AND EVALUATION

The picture which was described for marketing control is just reversed in production: German production managers have a much tighter grasp of production control than the British. As found often in this study, French managers fall in between.

To demonstrate this result, data similar to those used in marketing are described below: a list of eight quantitative operational production objectives and thirteen qualitative non-operational objectives was presented to production managers and they chose the five most important ones. Operational objectives included productivity, quantity produced, direct manufacturing costs, etc. Non-operational ones included adapting promptly to demand fluctuation, quality and adapting to new product introduction, to name but a few.

Table 7.1 indicates the number of each kind of objective cited as being among the five most important by production managers.

Operational Control: Marketing and Production

TABLE 7.11 Number of times operational and non-operational production objectives have been chosen in the first five[a]

	Great Britain	Germany	France
Qualitative non-operational	11	30	20
Quantitative operational	10	15	12
Total	21	45	32

[a] Only objectives for which the complete set of data on the control process was available are reported here or on roughly 60% of all objectives mentioned.

In the same fashion as in marketing, this result does not seem to be the consequence of some dominant set of objectives chosen by a particular country and different from that chosen in another country. In fact, quite a large number of objectives were selected among the twenty-one offered (around fifteen selected with no dominant pattern).

Parallel to the scenario developed in marketing, a shorter interval between performance measurements is associated with those managers (e.g., German) who have a tighter grasp on production control.

TABLE 7.12 Setting standards and measuring performance on qualitative non-operational production objectives

	Great Britain	Germany	France
Has standard[a] and is measured	0	21	10
Has no standards[b] and is not measured	7	8	3
Has no standards but is measured	4	1	7
Total	11	30	20

[a] Fisher p = ·001
[b] $\chi^2 = 13\cdot45$, df = 1, α = ·001 (Great Britain vs bloc of France and Germany).

TABLE 7.13 Time-span between production control measurements

	Great Britain %		Germany %		France %	
A day	4	17	14	35	2	6
Over a day	20	83	26	65	28	94
Total	24	100	40	100	30	100

The looser grasp of British managers in production control seems to be the result of the same type of process as in marketing: a higher executive further removed from those who have to achieve performance in setting standards and measuring, as illustrated by Tables 7.14 and 7.15.

The evaluation of production performance is a matter which can go up to top management, as with marketing. However, consistent with the emphasis put on production in Germany, it

TABLE 7.14 Who sets standards?

	Great Britain %	Germany %	France %
The production department itself	36	61	61
Outside the department (controller, chief executive)	64	39	39
Total	100	100	100

TABLE 7.15 Who measures performance?

	Great Britain %	Germany %	France %
The department itself	40	53	57
Outside the department	60	47	43
Total	100	100	100

Operational Control: Marketing and Production

TABLE 7.16 Who evaluates?

	Great Britain	Germany	France
	%	%	%
The department itself	52	33	70
Outside (controller, top management)	48	67	30
Total	100	100	100

goes more to the top there than in the two other countries (Table 7.16).

This table also indicates that in France, although production is also emphasised at the top, the closeness of supervision which seems to be required is not achieved (evaluation goes up to the top in only 30 per cent of the cases) — a further indication of the lack of differentiation in the formalism of control between marketing and production which has already been described at the beginning of the current chapter. French managers seem to favour centralisation in theory, but they keep information to themselves and informally feel themselves to be autonomous (57 per cent say so for production whereas only 25 per cent say so in Great Britain and Germany), which may indicate some degree of incoherence in French management. In descriptions of the French system one frequently finds an emphasis both on the heavily bureaucratic nature of the system and on how people strive to beat the system, through, for instance, the creation of reserved domains within which they may safeguard individualism. We will pursue this idea further in Part Three.

CONCLUSION: SOME INDICATIONS OF OPERATIONAL CONTROL EFFECTIVENESS

As a conclusion, the chief executives' subjective evaluations of the effectiveness of production and marketing control are presented in Table 7.17.

As may be seen the British do not seem very satisfied with their production controls and feel better about marketing. This corroborates the findings in terms of tighter grasp in marketing.

TABLE 7.17 Chief executives' subjective assessments of degrees of success in production and marketing control

	PRODUCTION CONTROL			MARKETING CONTROL		
	Great Britain	Germany	France	Great Britain	Germany	France
Very successful	0	2	2	3	0	2
Moderately successful	9	7	7	6	6	2
Very unsuccessful	2	4	3	4	7	9

The Germans have mixed feelings about their success in control activities, especially in the marketing area where seven out of thirteen feel very dissatisfied. This matches quite well with the operational difficulties in the marketing area. It might be a result of the lack of the organisational flexibility which is required in that area.

As for France, control seems to be better in production and not good at all in marketing (nine out of fourteen chief executives rate it as very unsuccessful). This might be due to the relative lack of differentiation from production control which was witnessed.

SUMMARY

The description of control practices at the operational level in marketing and production revealed three majors trends:

— First, a high consistency on a national basis on the objectives pursued in control which in turn reinforces the idea of differences across countries. For Great Britain, however, this consistency had to be qualified: operational managers use control more as a policing instrument than group top executives. It tends to demonstrate that control becomes less a guiding instrument and more a surveillance instrument as one gets nearer operations. The British structural

arrangements do not provide a close supervision of operations from the top; control is overall at that level. However at subsidiary level managers have to be more concerned about details if they want to get the job done.
- Secondly, marketing and production control differ in terms of the degree of formalism achieved, at least in Germany and Great Britain: production control is more formal than marketing control. This is quite coherent with the constraints and differences in objectives pursued in those two functions: production is more short-term and more technically oriented than marketing. However, within a given function, the degree of formalism is not achieved through the same means. In Germany, greater centralisation and lack of autonomy are the major factors which contribute to the higher formalism in production. In Great Britain, more formalism in production is attained through a higher frequency of performance measurement and the use of more comprehensive rules rather than a greater closeness of supervision. At all levels, then, the different degree of decentralisation in decision-making between the two countries seem to account for the way control is practised.
- Thirdly, a tighter grasp is achieved in marketing control in Great Britain whereas a tighter grasp is achieved in production control in Germany. French practices fall in between with some inconsistencies. With respect to the process by which a tighter grasp is achieved, it seems that, in both functions, the ability to set proper standards and measure performance frequently enough necessitates a large degree of autonomy in the control process at least at the monitoring stage — even if evaluation can go high up in the hierarchy to be able to grasp non-operational objectives. Thus, too great an involvement of top management hinders operational managers in the task of setting up proper standards and proper measurement devices for those objectives which are not immediately quantifiable.

The strong emphasis and commitment concerning production matters in Germany is thus further demonstrated at the operational level. In return the emphasis on operational efficiency which was previously indicated may diminish some of the flexibility needed in marketing. British managers on the contrary seem to be more committed to flexibility in their structure and planning and more market-oriented, which in turn may account for their relatively more efficient marketing control. As for France, one may be surprised by the lack of tightness in production control. Similar characteristics seem to link French practices to the German system. Still, the internal logic is not pushed as far. As a result, several inconsistencies have appeared in operational control. True, the corporate commitment and emphasis is on production. However, at the operational level too much autonomy seems to be allowed. This may be due to an overconfidence of chief executives towards their production managers (same background and training). Alternatively, there may be a lack of complete involvement on the part of top management in production, afraid as they are to jeopardise whatever equilibrium they have achieved in plants faced with potential social unrest and very strong trade union activism in France. The reasoning for chief executives may be to avoid making harsh decisions at the top level so as to keep a low profile in normal times *vis-à-vis* activist unions who today have 'les Patrons' (the bosses) as a target, and also to be able to step in with added effect in the case of social unrest.

Now that all differences and similarities in control practices have been described, emphasising across-countries comparisons, the research turns in Part Three to explanations both from country factors and from management theory factors. Each type will be discussed in turn and propositions derived from the measurement of the relative impact of each factor will be presented.

Part Three

Analysing Management Control Practices

8 Influences Contributing to Differences in Control Practices Between Countries

SCOPE OF CHAPTER

This chapter and the next one bring in explanations of the described detailed management control practices and conclude with propositions. Clearly the data show some overlapping in practices between countries although differences are quite sharp. 'Cultural explanations' are thus important but not sufficient. The close relationship seen between planning structure and control, for instance, shows that resorting only to country factors for explanation will not be enough. The next chapter will bring in both impacts on selected features of control, while this one focuses on country factors only, as it draws on secondary sources only. A summary of the findings across countries is first presented. The central question answered in this chapter is: 'What lies behind the observed differences in control practices by country?' What plausible explanations may be advanced to account for these differences? The discussion draws heavily on secondary sources and is consequently frankly speculative.

SUMMARY OF COUNTRY DIFFERENCES IN CONTROL PRACTICES WITHIN THEIR CONTEXTUAL (Structure and Planning) FRAMEWORK

Tables 8.1 and 8.2 summarise the differences seen in context (structure and planning) and in control practices between Great Britain, Germany and France.

148   Top Management Control in Europe

TABLE 8.1   Country differences in structure and planning

1. British structure is somewhat flexible, oriented towards autonomous product-market units in a holding company framework with a limited central staff and a high level of decentralisation in decision-making. Bottom-up strategic and long-range planning are emphasised as well as annual budgets.
2. The German structure, either functional or divisional, is pyramidal, somewhat rigid, and relies on a large central staff. Many decisions are centralised. Planning is oriented towards operational efficiency through project programming and medium-range operations planning.
3. The French structure is mainly functional; although tending towards the German characteristics, it is less formalised. Long-range planning is mistrusted and not used much. Coordination is infrequent.

TABLE 8.2   Country differences in control practices

1. British top control is less frequent and detailed. It is oriented towards financial matters and quite effective in that area. Production control is less emphasised and less successful. Marketing control works better. Control is used much more as a guiding instrument than a recording device. It relies heavily on line management self control and is done by hand, rather than relying on centralised computerised data.
2. German control is more frequent and detailed. It is oriented towards operational efficiency and production and is effective here. It relies on short term programming and necessitates heavy central machinery. Self control is not the rule. Control is often still viewed as a surveillance rather than a guiding instrument. Systematic and automated, it is not so successful in marketing and people seem to resent such surveillance. However new tendencies appear in the move from '*Kontrolle*' to 'Controlling'.
3. French control is in between, leaning towards the German system with less systematicness and much less effectiveness. Except among a modern minority, it is viewed as a recording instrument often not preceded by adequate planning.
4. In all three countries there is a lack of strategic control at the top managerial level.

SECONDARY SUPPORT FOR TREATING COUNTRY DIFFERENCES SERIOUSLY

As may be seen from the two previous tables and the descriptive material presented in Part Two, on many aspects of control the

German and British systems are the most divergent, whereas French control practices usually fall in between, although leaning heavily towards Germany.

The question arises as to which specific educational, cultural or economic factors might best explain these cross-country differences. These factors, offered as a scanning net in Chapter 2, however, must be complemented by a fourth one uncovered during the research: control practice seems to vary significantly according to whether the company is headed by a professional manager or is family-managed. This variable included in the analysis as representing the structure of industry in each country, may have broader implications when one looks at other countries where family businesses may be dominant (e.g. less-developed nations).

In trying to relate the findings to specific factors in each country the researcher feels more comfortable in presenting potential sources of explanation for each country separately in order to better identify key causal factors taken from secondary sources. They must necessarily be regarded as speculative explanations as they relate the data of this research (on the fifty-two companies) to broader findings of other researchers. Thus, they must be looked at with caution and are offered as plausible hypotheses.

GREAT BRITAIN

British control practices are typified by a low degree of detailed control from the top, a financial emphasis, high autonomy together with trust and reliance on subordinates, a stronger orientation towards the future than the past, a more extensive use of exception principles at the top and a better grasp of marketing control than production control.

These control traits seem to be quite consistent with the type of organisational arrangements and planning process found in these firms. In fact, the degree of decentralisation in decision-making is often a key factor in the control practices.

One may venture several types of explanation, such as the educational backgrounds of managers, the economic conditions prevailing in Great Britain and cultural traits of the British people.

(a) On the *educational* level, it has been said many times that British managers generally have been trained in the arts and that their initial aim was to work in the civil service:

> In Britain, many undergraduates taking arts subjects realise only at the last moment they are likely to go to industry. Like reluctant maidens, they go to a shotgun wedding, putting aside their tender thoughts of the Foreign Service, the *Guardian* and the BBC.[1]

This may account in large part for the reluctance of top managers to deal with technical matters and their greater ability to comprehend financial and marketing matters, production being more technology-loaded than finance and marketing. In turn marketing and to a lesser degree finance is more 'arts-like'.

Often British industry is characterised as having been the first to participate in the industrial revolution of the nineteenth century but having failed to renew itself and reinvest in new technologies. One also describes the strengths of British industries as being much more in the services (travel, newspapers), in the financial area (banks, insurance) and in trade rather than in purely technical matters. These various facts may be causes of the lack of technical orientation which in turn leads to less emphasis on the production or R & D sides of the firm.

(b) As for the impact of *economic conditions*, several factors are worth mentioning. To start with, the British economy has been recently plagued by high inflation and restrictions imposed on the British to fight it. It may therefore not come as a surprise that, on the control side, the emphasis has been on working-capital management and generation of cash. As a plausible complementary explanation, a high rate of inflation also means revising projections frequently, which we have often seen being done in Britain (the 'now-expected figures' syndrome; see page 00).

In fact, results can be very seriously affected by rapidly changing conditions in both the domestic and international markets if one does not update data.

Under these same economic conditions, managers' as well as workers' living standards have not been very good in recent years. Phases I and II of the latest government anti-inflation programme severely restricted consumption and income by increasing taxes tremendously on high income and curbing wage increases.

This may have two consequences for control. Either it may become difficult to motivate people to work up to objectives other than by sheer persuasion if monetary incentives are not available, or it may become necessary instead to increase non-monetary fringe benefits or intrinsic rewards. One such intrinsic reward involves appointing people as managing directors. Others include such perquisites as company cars, expense accounts, etc., and thus require more autonomy.

This preoccupation was voiced many times by the executives interviewed: 'We cannot motivate by extra cash benefits; thus we have a heavy brain drain of talented people. The only way is to provide fringe benefits.'

The themes of current humour may offer some insight. A recent 'tongue in cheek' article in the *Herald Tribune* concerning company in-house lunches in Great Britain concludes that such lunches are bringing the fatal blow to the British economy.[2] As another directly assessed indication, in annual reports of the firms investigated and where top executives' compensation have to be published, it is rare to see salaries above $40,000 a year.

In such economic conditions, with such weak incentives for going into industry, one may wonder about the ability of the British system to stimulate managerial skills.

Some executives mentioned compensating for the lack of financial rewards by taking an outside job such as consulting. This sharing of attentions may assuage an executive's need for higher income, but it is doubtful that it is of any help to the company.

(c) As for the impact of *'cultural traits'* on control, the concept of 'gifted amateurs' (see D. Granick, for instance[3]), often depicted as typical of British enterprise, may also well explain why managers are generally not very close to operations. As one chief executive told the researcher:

When Mr X was still chief executive and main stockholder, and we were discussing some serious problem in the board room, he used to say, 'Let's deal with it like gentlemen'. You recognise a gentleman by looking under his shoes; if the hollow in the sole just in front of the heel is polished then he is a gentleman.

Another more cultural reason may be one identified in the Haire et al.[4] study, which showed that British and U.S. managers represented a cluster of countries (Anglo-Saxon) that differed significantly from the Nordic European (part of which is Germany) and the Latin European (part of which is France) clusters in their beliefs about individual capacity for initiative and leadership. This may be an alternative explanation for the holding company structure which in turn has led to autonomy in control at operational level.

Throughout the interviews, the researcher was impressed by the willingness and determination with which British chief executives wanted to delegate and give autonomy. On many occasions, their commitment to decentralisation principles was probed by showing the chief executive some advantages of more centralised decisions and tasks – What about having the same trade name? What about R & D synergies? What about common personnel or training policies? What about moving managers around within the group? What about centralised purchasing? The answers were invariably that autonomy had to be left to operations. Furthermore, it was thought that the individual subsidiaries, often acquired, were better known to customers than the holding company. This advantage would be eroded if too much integration occurred. The general feeling was also that the holding structure synergy was to be essentially financial – namely how to maximise the use of resources – that everywhere in control self-control was the rule, except in money matters. It led one chief executive to say:

> We took over a textile company that was losing money. We felt that by tightening money supply, by requiring cash remittance and cash generation, by increasing working capital we could turn out profits. We did so in less than a year. Money is the key.

Also mentioned quite often was the desire to leave to the managing director a freedom to manage (by giving him a top title together with a directorship for his immediate subordinates on the subsidiary's board) which would motivate them more than being simple executives in an integrated group.

Following this philosophy, long-range planning is often a bottom-up approach where corporate strategy is often a mere aggregation of product-market unit plans.

In fact, when top management has tried to centralise an area, it results in a loss of grasp in control by the line. This is especially true in production, where it was seen that standard setting measurement and evaluation tended to get centralised and resulted in a looser control over non-operational qualitive objectives.

According to the previous comments, one could thus tend to relate British control practices to the low inclination of British managers to concentrate on technical matters; the necessity of controlling financial resources during rapid inflation; the tradition of trade which means the marketing area is grasped better; the necessity of providing managers with non-monetary rewards which leads to a decentralised structure; and, finally, the belief of the British in the individual's capacity for initiative and leadership which has led to decentralisation and control autonomy.

GERMANY

German control is typified by a high degree of detailed control information sent up to top management, an emphasis on production and operational efficiency together with a lower trust and reliance on subordinates, a better grasp of production control than marketing control, a heavy use of central comprehensive information systems – often computerised – and a high degree of formalism.

These control traits are quite consistent with the organisational arrangements and planning processes involved: specialisation, centralised management styles and detailed specific one-year plans. However, in Germany control took two different – often opposing – forms: *'Kontrolle'* and *'Controlling'*. One must thus also try to see whether these two types are used by firms with different characteristics: the family versus professional management hypothesis has to be closely examined here.

On the whole the first explanation that comes to mind concerns the beliefs and attitudes of management in Germany.

Cultural traits

The discipline, efficiency and preference of Germans for neat organisational settings have often been described as dominant cultural traits. Following this view, one would tentatively find it quite consistent that the consequence in terms of control is a search for efficiency by setting key tasks and objectives, and that a well-compartmentalised structure leads to a high formalism in management, particularly in the control system. Reliance on hard facts (quantitative data preferred) may stem from the same sources. Finally, a lack of the flexibility often required in marketing results in a less tight grasp of that function in German firms.

Another leading explanation offered in studies of German management has stressed its authoritarian style.[5] This in turn means much more centralism in designing control systems and objectives and in measuring and evaluating performance.

A third more general cultural explanation may be similar to the one expressed by Henri C. Wallich:

> In many cases this compulsive urge to work seems to be connected with a sense of insecurity that some observers regard as a basic German characteristic. Whatever the causes, which the sufferer is normally unaware of, he finds intensive work an excellent antidote. It enables him to lose himself and its material rewards fortify him against some of his troubles. Success alleviates inferiority feelings and promises security and happiness for the future.[6]

It has been suggested that this was one important reason for the appearance of a new group of businessmen after the war; people got involved in business to get out of an unpleasant post-war situation.

In addition, as noted by Harbison and Myers,[7] the German chief executive has a 'high status role [especially as] many are owner executives, which means there is a gulf between the man at the top and the lower managerial ranks'.

Both indications could reasonably shed some light on the high degree of centralisation and authoritarian styles perceived, as well as for the emphasis on efficiency.

Authority, discipline, sense of organisation and emphasis on

Differences in Control Practices 155

efficiency in turn mean not leaving any loose ends. Reporting all variances will be preferred to reporting only the most important ones or to selecting key figures for top management attention as in Great Britain; detailed objectives will be preferred to overall ones; full costing to marginal costing.

Owner-entrepreneurs versus professional management

There is a changing pattern emerging, however, in German management, as noted by S. Grosset.[8] Pre-war German industry was dominated by powerful families; in the post-war reconstruction new educated entrepreneurs not belonging to those families emerged. Although borrowing the same authoritarian principles, these are more professional managers motivated to do the best job. This may well explain the fact that two concepts of control work in parallel. Family-owned, founder- and/or family-managed companies have not yet accepted new concepts of control such as guiding (*steuern*). They rely more on close supervision and cost accounting.

In the other cases, highly trained newcomers do not hesitate to bring in external professional management: 'In most cases, the accession of newcomers, though not breaking the old class barrier, has brought about duality in the group of executives.'[9]

Economic conditions

As a complementary explanation, one may stress the high growth-rate and low inflation of the German economy. An executive joking about increasing productivity when the Deutschmark went up illustrates the stress on sticking to plan, on controlling production costs to stay competitive in international markets.

In summary, the authoritarian German managerial style reported by Hartmann[10] is still present and dominant. It leads to detailed control from the top and centralised information systems. Business efficiency and rationalisation are favoured by German managers. Although this is not new, it may have been reinforced by the sense of guilt of the last world war. However, the post-war period has seen the creation of a new breed of entrepreneurs, highly skilled in their managerial behaviour and in the techniques used.

FRANCE

What explains French management control practices which in most instances follow the German style but with less formalism, less sophistication and sometimes less coherence? Although at first glance the French sub-sample may appear biased with respect to the presence of owner-entrepreneurs, it may in fact be reasonably representative of French reality and depict the overall bias of this French reality as compared to what prevails in Great Britain or Germany.

Overall, thus, French control practices tend towards a high degree of detail at the top management level, high centralism in control and heavy emphasis on production control. However, as compared to the British and German reality, both control and planning systems are much less advanced and sophisticated.

One may offer comparable sources of explanation for this entire set of attitudes.

Education

The educational backgrounds of managers in France clearly show the predominance of technical training. Over two thirds of top managers come from engineering whereas it is less than one third in Great Britain. This high representation of engineers coming mostly from the *grandes écoles* is certainly causal to the emphasis on production control. However, one may also argue that this has been given too much emphasis. Chief executives who come from *Polytechnique* will trust anybody else coming from *Polytechnique*. As a result, because they come from the same prestigious educational backgrounds, production managers are the ones who obtain so much autonomy (noted in Chapter 7) that the grasp of control is loosened in that area.[11]

Technical background is not the only distinctive educational trait of French managerial personnel. As noted by several authors, the Cartesian bias of the French educational system causes some problems in terms of pragmatic problem-solving:

> The French approach is Cartesian, and stands for the most systematic and quantitative assault possible on every problem while taking into consideration all factors which may influence it. Thus if the same problem is presented to a French

Differences in Control Practices

and to an American businessman the former is liable to discover, say, twenty factors which influence it and think about fifty alternative solutions. The American by contrast would probably look for the three main factors.[1,2]

If a control system is not comprehensive enough to permit monitoring every event, then it is felt not to be worthwhile: it has loopholes.

Until 'all facets, all alternatives, all consequences' types of control systems are found which involve massive computer requirements and are called *la Gestion intégrée* (integrated management), one does not trust them and prefers to rely on the informal methods of control which were found in many French firms.

Cultural traits

However, when such systems are found, they then become part of the 'bureaucratic' French organisation[13] as described by the marketing manager of one of the firms studied:

> Why do you ask me about control? It is not my job any more. The controller's office has put to work a comprehensive system using the computer. I do not deal with control. He does. It is so comprehensive that I do not feel motivated to look at the data and see if something is wrong; at any rate he will do it. Why should I bother?

Thus, insistence on perfection (Cartesian mode) is countervailed by a disregard when it becomes perfect (too bureaucratic). Inconsistencies such as this one are not only obvious at the operational level but also at the top management level. Some firms studied in the sample are quite famous in France for their chief executives' involvement and speeches on the human side of the firm. They advocate the creation of decentralised – both geographically and administratively – operating units (mainly production ones) instead of massive production units: they call these units 'human-sized' (*taille humaine*). However, many studies and observations show the overall lack of trust of managers in their subordinates,[14] the high level of centralisation[15] as well as the low rate of accountability they are ready to require in terms of performance.

For that matter, authors have suggested[16] that one of the main differences between American and European management — Germany excepted — is the difference in ideology: Europeans and typically French managers feel guilty about business and profits. Thus rigid commitments to plans and projected income statements are not considered as important as getting along well with others.

Another trait of French managerial attitudes is the charismatic, autocratic role of the chief executive. This has been expressed[17] as an explanation for the lack of decentralisation in both France and Germany. In Germany, however, the new post-war *unternehmers* seem to come from a different breed, and in the executive office responsibility seems to be more widely shared among the members of the *Vorstand* — or at least this seemed to be the case in the professionally managed firms investigated. In France, on the contrary, the chief executive — who is also chairman of the board — is in all cases more of a loner. As an example, two of the firms investigated had chosen the German legal entity — a council of surveillance and a *Vorstand (conseil de surveillance et directoire*[18]*)*. In those two cases, the *President du Directoire* was a majority stockholder and his two colleagues did not begin to be his equals in power and decision-making authority.

This charismatic, autocratic role of the chief executive may be in a cause of the lower degree of formalism in French control.

Although the French are described as bureaucratic — which would normally lead to very formal written systems — chief executives at their level prefer to rely on direct oral control. In that way, they can bypass the hierarchy and take whatever decisions they wish as the sole last representatives of charismatic power, whereas their subordinates would be required to use formal rules.

The French — and Latin — propensity for individualism may be ventured as an explanation of why the logic of the German control system is not applied as well in France. It has for instance been reported that, compared to Anglo-Saxon or German managers, French managers are less inclined to have informal oral exchanges.[19] Case methods which require teamwork do not work very well in France. Again bureaucratic tendencies may well be counteracted by the creation of reserved domains for individuals. This in turn prevents people from sharing much information thereby keeping their options open.

(c) *Professional managers versus entrepreneurs*

As in Germany, there seem to be two philosophies of management, depending on whether the firm is headed by the founder or his family, or by professional managers who do not have a large stake in the firm. The tendency for owners will be to require more detailed, less sophisticated, less formal control and to have a heavier involvement in operations than professionally oriented managers (see Appendix E). As in Germany, there seem to be at least two business elites (see the work of Savage on profiles of French top managers[20]). The characteristics of these two elites are quite different. The owners are much more involved in operational control, much less inclined to delegate, and rely much more on cost accounting than management control. Although the average degree of decentralisation in French firms was low when compared with Great Britain (see Chapter 4), there was a large spread. This would suggest the presence of at least a minority of modern managers; this presence was also felt during the interviews. In this minority, delegation was higher, cost accounting played a lesser role; modern planning and control systems with transfer prices between marketing and production units were likely to be in effect; budgets were the rule.

In summary, to attempt to explain why French control practices are near German ones, but less systematic, several factors were presented. The heavy emphasis on engineering in educational backgrounds was felt to be causal to production control emphasis. The Cartesian education was felt to lead to the split between formal centralised control and intuitive personal control. The French tendency for bureaucracy can be contrasted with weak control of operations when a fully rationalised system cannot be established. The charismatic role of chief executives also helps to explain why control is in fact less formalised and more oral. A lack of trust in subordinates and lack of delegation explained the nature of detailed controls at the top. This was counteracted by the creation of reserved domains on lower levels which express a tendency to try to preserve individualism typical of French society. Finally, as in Germany, the presence of two business elites was offered as an explanation for the different degrees of sophistication witnessed in control systems.

SUMMARY

Tenatative explanations have been proposed to account for the differences in control practices witnessed between countries. No attempt has been made at a full description of cultural impact, but the apparent connection between the conclusions of other studies of the countries and the observed differences in control practices reinforces the conclusion that such differences are fundamental. Cultural traits – such as beliefs and attitudes towards authority – often selected as unique explanatory factors in comparative research are not, however, the only potential factors. Current economic conditions and managers' educational backgrounds as well as the difference between family and professional management seem to play a concomitant role.

With these tentative descriptive summaries in mind, further analysis of these patterns and suggestions for further research will be presented in the next chapter. It will discuss management theory's relative impact and then combine the two in order to introduce propositions which suggest a reconciliation of two theories – namely the culture-bound school of comparative management and the universalist school of management – and directions for further research.

NOTES

1. M. Ivens, 'Behind the Organization Man', *Twentieth Century*, vol. 17, no. 3 (Spring 1965) pp. 21–2.
2. *International Herald Tribune* (14 February 1978).
3. D. Granick, *The European Executive* (New York: Doubleday, 1962).
4. M. Haire, E. E. Ghiselli and L. W. Porter, *Managerial Thinking* (New York: John Wiley, 1966).
5. H. Hartmann, *Authority and Organization in German Management* (Princeton, N.J.: Princeton University Press, 1959); Nowothny, 'American vs European Management Philosophy', *Harvard Business Review* (March–April 1964), pp. 101–8.
6. H. C. Wallich, *Mainsprings of the German Revival* (New Haven, Conn.: Yale University Press, 1955), p. 333.

7. F. Harbison and C. A. Myers, *Management in the Industrial World* (New York: McGraw Hill, 1959) p. 129.
8. S. Grosset, *Management, European and American Styles* (Belmont, Calif.: Wadsworth Publishing Co., 1970).
9. 'Germany's New Business Man', *The Economist* (1 August 1964) pp. 485–6.
10. H. Hartmann, op. cit.
11. See D. Granick, *Managerial Comparisons of Four Developed Countries: France, Great Britain, United States and Russia* (Cambridge, Mass.: MIT Press, 1972), p. 206. Although German chief executives may have the same technical orientations, as top management is collegial, a more balanced approach might be found. For a comparable study in Germany, see W. Stahl: *Der Elitereislauf in der Unternehmerschaft* (Frankfurt/M.: Verlag Harri Deutsch, 1973), pp. 232–4; Heinrich Evers, *Kriterien Zur Auslese von Top Managern in Großunternehmen: Eine Empirische Untersuchung* (Frankfurt/M.: Harri Deutsch, 1974).
12. T. D. Weinschall, 'Communication, Culture and the Education of Multinational Managers', in T. D. Weinschall (ed.), *Culture and Management* (Harmondsworth, Middlesex: Penguing Books, 1977) p. 172.
13. Michel Crozier, *The Bureaucratic Phenomenon* (Chicago: University of Chicago Press, 1964).
14. See for instance M. Haire *et al.*, op. cit.
15. D. Granick, op. cit.
16. See for instance Francois Bourricaud, 'Sociologie du Chef d'Entreprise: le Jeune Patron', *Revue Economique*, vol. 6 (November 1958), pp. 896–911.
17. See for instance J. R. Pitts, 'The Bourgeois Family and French Economic Retardation', PhD thesis (Boston: Harvard University, 1957); G. X. Trepo, 'The Introduction of Management by Objectives in France: Reality of Ritual?' Doctoral thesis (Boston: Harvard Business School, 1971).
18. This legal form is acceptable in both countries as it has been selected as the EEC European legal form for corporations.
19. See for instance T. D. Weinshall, 'Communication, Culture and the Education of Multinational Managers', in T. D. Weinschall (ed.), op. cit., p. 167; see also Michel Crozier, op. cit.
20. D. Savage, 'Les Dirigeants et la Croissance des Entreprises', *Sociologie du Travail*, vol. 2 (February–April 1975).

9 Emerging Propositions Regarding Differences in Management Control Practices

SCOPE OF CHAPTER

The purpose of this chapter is to distill from this exploratory study a set of tentative propositions, or hypotheses, which seem to explain much of the difference in control practices in the three countries.

It is necessarily tentative but in view of the complete absence of in-depth empirical data in this field a series of field-based propositions is needed. Although links to existing theories will be noted, the propositions are primarily based on an analysis of the data compiled in this study.

The mere fact that significant differences were often found between countries should not satisfy the researcher that 'country' is the only explanation of those differences.

With respect to those other variables two classes were identified: 'business variables' which include the impact of strategy, market stability and technological complexity (sector) on control, and 'management system' variables or the influence of organisation structure and planning on control. In addition professionalism, uncovered during the research, is included in the analysis.

STATISTICAL SCANNING FOR SIGNIFICANT IMPACTS ON CONTROL PRACTICES

In order to sort out these impacts, the management control practices previously described in much detail must, for practical purposes, be somewhat aggregated into indexes summarising key features which have been selected as representative of control from the total corporation's — or at least top management's — point of view:

1. The degree of detail in control (i.e., how much top management formal control systems go into details as well as how much information goes to the top).
2. The frequency of control (i.e., how often chief executives look at performance).
3. The degree of formalism in control (i.e., how much emphasis is given to written material in control).
4. The degree of centralism in control (i.e., how much is done centrally and how much is left for self control to managers).
5. The degree of sophistication in control (i.e., the degree of use of control as a guiding future-oriented instrument rather than a simple recording device as well as the degree to which modern techniques are used).
6. The emphasis of control (i.e., which functions get most attention by chief executives).

Two features from the operational level were also summarised in index form:

1. The key characteristics of control (i.e., how formalised and quantified operational control is).
2. The frequency of control (i.e., how frequent operational control is).

To minimise any potential cultural bias which might stem from the respondents' discrepant perceptions of opinion questions, in the vast majority of cases only *factual* data were taken into account in the index-building process.

Table 9.1 below summarises — when they are not self-explanatory from the previous paragraph — how these data-based indexes have been built (mostly on ordinal scales).

However, it must be pointed out that the aggregation performed does not encompass all the richness, breadth and depth of the information gathered Each interview guideline was thirty pages long; altogether 400 different informations were collected. In addition content analysis of each company's documents (on

TABLE 9.1   Control indexes

TOP MANAGEMENT

Degree of detail on top management control:

> presence and number of daily weekly information looked at by chief executives
> time devoted to control
> content of reports: everything or key results; detailed costs or not; all variances or key variances
> approval needed for actual spending of capital expenditures
> number of items on which cost accounting bear.

Degree of formalism in top management control:

> written organigram (a proxy)
> request for qualitative report sent with monthly quantitative reports
> number of items in the monthly report
> formal signature before actual spending of capital budgets.

Degree of autonomy of managers in control (or centralism):

> control thought to be top management on everybody's job
> who sends report to CEO (line or central staff or both)
> degree of involvement of central staff in preparing reports
> rated influence of line managers in setting objectives.

Degree of sophistication in control:

> length of time since company has cost accounting, budgets, profit centres
> basis for setting targets (future or past)
> types of budgets
> use of control techniques

OPERATIONAL LEVEL

Formalism of control:

> frequency
> specificity of review
> check on subordinate's decisions
> formality of link between results of control and rewards
> specificity of criteria for evaluation of an individual
> degree of use of rules in control.

Frequency

> — frequency of performance measurement for each of five most important objectives.

structure, planning and control) also added to the depth of analysis. The data-collection process was clearly oriented towards obtaining an overall feel, in as 'deep' and detailed a fashion as possible, for the reality of control practices.

Furthermore, it must be remembered that five key dimensions of control were examined (*Functions* such as marketing, production, finance; *organisation* such as top management, division or functions, *time horizon, elements* − (strategic control, long-range, etc.) − and *characteristics* − formal, detailed). Part Two gave an overall picture of these dimensions and the many possible combinations of features from one dimension to another. For practical purposes (i.e., to reduce testing for relationships with independent variables, and also because of the researcher's feeling of the representativeness of the indexes of the reality seen) only one dimension of control is discussed in the analysis presented here, namely the characteristics of control.

The 'independent variables' (i.e. 'business variables' and 'management system' variables) were also quantified on ordinal scale as shown in Table 9.2.

In order to relate these aggregated 'dependent variables' to the previously described 'independent variables' and assess the degree of association, two types of analysis have been used.

The first one consisted in assessing the degree of association of each dependent variable with each independent variable by means of non-parametric correlation analysis.

The size of the sample and the use of relatively weaker forms of quantification (i.e. the level of measurement being mostly nominal or ordinal) do not warrant attaching much significance to narrow differences in correlation coefficients. Consequently, correlation analysis was primarily used to sort out major impacts. (Also, for those reasons, the degree of confidence was set relatively high at .05, and in most cases, when they existed, associations were significant at .01 or better.)

Once sorted out, these associations were checked by contingency tables. In that process, further aggregation was needed because of the small size of the sample. In order not to aggregate those tables too much, each feature of control was set at three levels (high, medium, low). Because of potential errors of measurement built into the index construction, only the frequencies in the high and low category were used and a Fisher test was applied. As this test presents the advantage of

166 Top Management Control in Europe

TABLE 9.2 Indexes for independent variables

'BUSINESS VARIABLES'

Strategy:
  degree of diversification (Standard Industrial Classification Index used and checked with chief executives comments on diversification)
  growth (as measured by sales over last three years), divided in three terciles: high, medium and low, and checked for equivalence from one country to another by inflation rates.

Market and technology (sector):
  electronics (high complexity, rapid changes)
  mechanical engineering (medium complexity and change)
  textiles (low complexity and change).

MANAGEMENT SYSTEM VARIABLES

Structure
  type (functional, divisional, holding or from low product-market coordination, heavy central staff, high specialisation to high production-market coordination, light central staff, low specialisation)
  degree of decentralisation (scores computed on chief executives' ratings of where seven key decisions where taken).

Planning:
  degree of sophistication score (existence of written long-range plan, encompassing or not strategic and structure dimensions, with or without planning manual.)

PROFESSIONALISM
  degree of domination of founder or family both financially and managerially.

---

computing the *exact probability* of occurrence of differences when in fact there is no difference, each can be more safely used and at least ranked from the most important to the least important when several independent variables are associated with a dependent variable. Probabilities under ·10 were the only ones retained.

To permit focus on important results,' the overall results of the statistical analysis are summarised in Table 9.3. This table shows — for each feature control characteristic selected through the index-building process — the significant relationships with one or several independent variables. By significant we mean that an independent variable had to correlate significantly with the feature of control selected at a level of ·05 or better *and*

Propositions on Differences in Control Practices 167

have a Fisher exact probability on extreme cases less than ·10. Only the Fisher exact probabilities are reported and the independent variables listed according to the ranks of the probabilities (first the independent variable with the lowest probability . . .).

A MODEL FOR THE STUDY OF MANAGEMENT CONTROL PRACTICES

As may be seen from this table, there is a high influence (i.e., lower probabilities) of country on top management degree of detail, frequency, degree of centralism and emphasis in control. This in itself does not warrant turning to cultural explanations of control practices. However, statistical analysis and Part Two descriptive material show that country also exerts an influence on organising processes (type of structure and degree of decentralisation) and to a lesser degree on planning. This information, combined with all the control dimensions investigated but not included in the indexes, would seem to indicate the predominance, either directly or indirectly, of country influences on control thorugh structure and planning.

Furthermore, the level of professionalism is strongly associated with the degree of detail, frequency and formalism in control. In addition statistical analysis show that family management firms are fast-growers and less-diversified firms.

If we now turn to business variables, strategic dimensions (diversification and growth) affect organising processes in a certain way more than they affect control directly: thus diversification leads to divisionalisation of structure but its impact is far less important than country ($p = ·01$); we find more ($p = ·10$) difference of level of decentralisation between countries than between levels of diversification.

The impact of sector is visible in two ways. The table suggests that as one looks more at operational control rather than top management control, sector difference is the only independent variable to affect control. Also, when technology is less complex, planning is less sophisticated.

As for management system variables, when we look at the level of each independent variable in each country, structure and planning have a significant impact on the degree of detail, frequency, centralism and sophistication of top management control. In addition planning is more sophisticated in non-

TABLE 9.3 Overall relationships of control practices with country, business and management system variables

	KEY Explanatory variables		Identified relationships
TOP MANAGEMENT CONTROL			
Degree of detail	Country	(p = ·0133)	Control is more detailed in France and Germany than in Great Britain.
	Decentralisation	(p = ·0151)	More decentralised firms control in less detail at the top.
	Professionalism	(p = ·032)	Family management tends to control in more detail than professional management.
	Planning	(p = ·032)	Firms with more sophisticated planning tend to control less in detail at the top.
	Sector	(p = ·061)	Complex technologies and more unstable markets require less detail in control.
Frequency	Country	(p = ·001)	Control is more frequent in Germany and France than in Great Britain.
	Professionalism	(p = ·048)	Family managers tend to control more frequently.
	Planning	(p = ·05)	When planning is more sophisticated control is less frequent.
	Growth	(p = ·095)	High growth firms control more frequently.
Degree of formalism	Professionalism	(p = ·001)	Family management is less formal than professional management.

Propositions on Differences in Control Practices

Degree of centralism (or autonomy)	Country Planning Structure	(p = ·066) (p = ·082) (p = ·0836)	Control is more centralized in Germany and France than in Great Britain. When planning is more sophisticated, more autonomy in control is left. Product market structures (holding give more self control than functional or divisional ones.
Degree of sophistication	Planning Sector Structure	(p = ·001) (p = ·04) (p = ·069)	The more sophisticated planning is, the more sophisticated control is. More complex sector leads to more sophisticated control. More product market structures require more sophistication in control.
Emphasis	Country		British chief executives favour overall financial control. German and French managers prefer operational production oriented control.
OPERATIONS CONTROL			
Characteristics (formalism)	(Sector)[a]		(The control in electronics is less formal than in textile.)
Frequency	(Sector)[a]		(The control in electronics is less frequent than in textile.)

[a] Only significant correlations found; however Fisher tests does not allow to reject the null hypothesis.

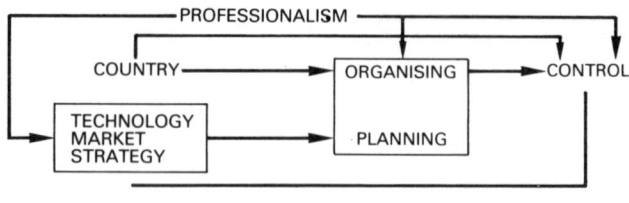

Fig. 9.1

functional structures than in functional ones irrespective of the sector and country (p = ·01).

These results would suggest the revised model (figure 9.1) of the influences which explain variations in management control practices from country to country.

PROPOSITIONS SUGGESTED FOR RESEARCH

1. THE DEBATE BETWEEN UNIVERSAL AND CULTURAL VIEW OF MANAGEMENT

This study focused on management control practices in France, Great Britain and Germany. However, it was felt necessary to embody in the research management concepts such as the impact of technology, management strategy and market environment on management processes and the impact of the interaction of management processes (i.e., impact of structure and planning) on control. These steps were necessary in order to be able to take the main findings and concepts of management theories and practices into account.

As a consequence, comparisons in control practices *per se* first have to be viewed in a broader context and tentatively answer the following question: to what extent are 'universal' management principles and theories applicable across countries and to what extent do the somewhat opposed claims of the 'cultural' school of comparative management hold true?

With respect to this question, evidence suggests a possible reconciliation between the universalist school of management and the hypotheses of the more culture-bound school of comparative management.

Support for the universal school of management comes mostly from the *direction* of changes in management processes.

Thus, the more complex the technology, the less detailed control is, whatever the country.

Support for the 'culture-bound' school of management comes mostly from the level of practices achieved. On the average decentralisation is higher in Great Britain than in the other two countries. As a result, the degree of detail in control is lower on the average than in the other two countries. Statistical analysis also shows that in Great Britain there is no correlation between the type of structure (functional, divisional, holding) and decentralisation scores. Whatever the structure, it also shows for the same country that the more we move towards free forms of structure (holding), the less formal operational controls become. This would suggest that in those free forms of structure headquarters — with its light staff — does not (and cannot) help local management in devising formal control systems. It could result in operational inefficiencies already noticed in production. Because in France — and to a lesser degree in Germany — there is resistance to giving autonomy through divisionalised structures, on average these structures are less often present and so also is sophistication in control. Because less autonomy is present, control is more a policing instrument than a guiding one.

Table 9.4 gives the most important universal relationships and whether they were found in each country.

This evidence suggests the following propositions:

The universalist school of management holds true mainly in so far as the direction of changes is concerned.

The culture-bound comparative school of management holds true mainly in so far as the level of practices is concerned.

This result suggests some qualifications regarding both schools of management. Whereas Koontz and O'Donnell asserted that in their view management principles and fundamentals are true the world over, this research suggests that they apply mainly to the way things are moving. However, although it is important to know in what direction to move when conditions are changing, it is just as important to assess what magnitude of proposed change is 'possible'. By 'possible' we mean to suggest that one has to evaluate the culture or country constraining or facilitating forces which will help or hinder the magnitude of management changes in order to achieve the desired results. In this respect,

TABLE 9.4 The universality issue (correlations with significance degree of ·05 or better)

Some universal principles	Great Britain	France	Germany
STRATEGY STRUCTURE			
Divisionalised (or holding) structures are more decentralised than functional structures	No	Yes	Yes
More decentralisation leads to more sophisticated planning	Reverse	No	Yes
Higher diversification leads to divisionalisation of structure[3]	Yes	No	No
Higher technology leads to more sophisticated planning	Yes	No	Yes
STRUCTURE PLANNING CONTROL			
Control is more sophisticated when planning is more sophisticated[2,4]	Yes	No	Yes
Control is more frequent, more detailed, less sophisticated in low technology such as textiles than in high technology such as electronics	Yes	Yes	Yes
Higher diversification requires more formal control	Yes	Yes	No
Higher diversification requires less detail in control from the top	Yes	No	No
Multiple structures lead to less detail in control from the top	Reverse	No	Yes
Decentralisation leads to more detail in control from the top[1]	Yes	No	No
Decentralization leads to more autonomy in control	Reverse	No	No

when people like Webber assert that management is culture-bound, they put too much emphasis on country variances with respect to beliefs and attitudes. In doing so, they deprive themselves of the benefits that a more general frame of reference can provide in making suggestions about the extent and rate of change.

2. INTERDEPENDENCY OF PLANNING, ORGANISATION STRUCTURE AND CONTROL IN EACH COMPANY'S MANAGEMENT SYSTEM

Evidence suggests that the different processes composing the management system of a firm are interdependent. On the one hand, structural characteristics affect control. For instance, in France the dominant functional organisation goes along with a greater emphasis on reporting to top management by functions rather than by products or markets. Use of large central staffs in Germany is associated with central and detailed reporting by divisions (by products, fixed costs, etc.). Decentralisation in decision-making is associated with less detail in control, etc.

On the other hand, planning and structure are also interdependent. Thus in multiform structure (divisions, holding) evidence suggests that planning is more sophisticated.

Finally, planning and control are also interdependent. Thus the results show that, generally speaking, more sophisticated planning leads to more sophisticated control.

The necessary interdependence and coherence in management design has been noted normatively in management literature[5,6] as a key to good implementation of a firm's strategy and the data reinforce this idea of interdependence. This should render us cautious when field studies are carried out on only one specific issue. It is stated as a first proposition:

> The interdependency between structure, planning and control calls for integrated research when focusing on one question pertaining to any one of those processes.

The interdependence just noted, however, has to be qualified with respect to current management literature. Whereas evidence suggests that the directions of associations are in some cases coherent with current concepts, other evidence uncovered problems which have not been so widely treated. In the first category one should list the following findings:

> Generally speaking, the more decentralised a firm, the less detailed control is at the top.

> The more sophisticated planning is, the more sophisticated control is; without adequate planning, control is less a guiding instrument and more a matter of surveillance

In the second category (i.e., not usually covered or contrary to normative management literature), the following propositions emerge from the data. With respect to planning and controls, the normatively defined sequence, according to which planning comes first and then control, might in fact have to be reversed.

Some form of control is necessary in order to develop planning instruments which in turn lead to adjusted controls.

This proposition is grounded in several empirical pieces of evidence. In Germany, for instance, *Kontrolle* — which means keeping records of past performance by products, markets, departments — has been, prior to controlling, a guiding instrument relying much less on fiscal or cost accounting and often an activity which embodies not only control but also planning. In France, in a company thinking of introducing planning, the controller has stated as its first task the development of an information basis for standards per department. More generally most French companies use control, although not all of them do planning. The suggested sequential steps might be as follows:

Fiscal accounting → cost accounting → managerial accounting → budgetary control → need for one-year plans and objectives → need for long-range plans → need for adjusted controls (i.e., not just budgetary control but control for each type of plan).

Also barely-covered in the literature and witnessed in the companies studied is the fact that top management, especially diversified firms, controls either at the planning stage or is solely reliant on short term information rather than control of strategic factors. It can be stated in the following fashion:

Top management control can be exercised at the planning stage, especially in diversified firms, but tools are often lacking; or it can be done at the doing stage but strategic control is not used.

In Great Britain, for instance, most of the strategic and long-term planning is prepared by the units. Then each unit presents its plan at headquarters in the presence of the chief executive, financial director and planning director (when there is one). At this stage, with sufficient time devoted to it, the chief executive has the opportunity to probe, to question the plans, to persuade the managing directors of other goals. This phase is repeated twice. Once accepted the plan is transformed into a budget with key sales, profit and cash objectives. Because of the mere size of the units, and also because the budget gives all main results, less detail in control is then needed from the top. As a company becomes more diversified the chief executive increases his reliance on planning discussions at subsidiary board meetings. Thus, control by the top is exercised at the planning stage and then autonomy for implementation is given to the line.

However, besides these formal meetings, no specific tools are used to probe the plans.

In France, when no planning exists the chief executive, not knowing where the firm is going, often becomes very anxious, knowing the daily sales and deliveries but wondering about the possible corrective actions. Thus, unable to control at the planning stage ('steering controls') he controls only with the aid of detailed short-term information.

If, however, control at the planning stage is difficult, top management could concentrate on monitoring strategic factors when the plan is implemented, monitoring the main hypotheses underlying plans, checking that key competences are developed as defined. However, no evidence of such strategic control has appeared although it is at least conceptually present.[7]

There is evidence of some explicit strategic planning or thinking at least from operations to headquarters. We may regard strategic planning as the highest and most recently developed level of all types of planning and especially suited to corporate top management. If one believes that a plan necessitates a control, then there is a gap to be filled in that area, as shown in figure 9.2.

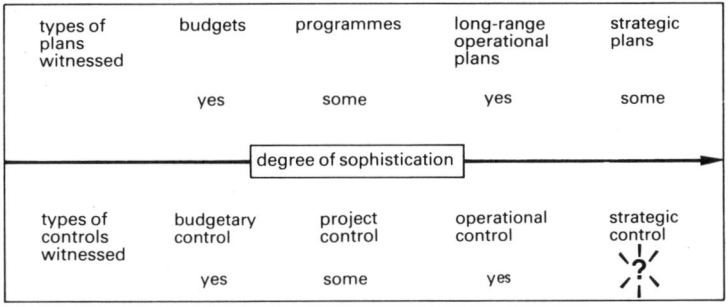

FIG. 9.2 Evolution of planning and control

3. EFFECT OF PROFESSIONALISATION

Evidence which suggests a relationship between professionalisation acting directly on control and indirectly through strategy, leads to the following propositions:

> Family-managed firms tend to be characterised by more rapid growth and less diversification than professionally managed firms.

In all three countries the high-growth firms were in fact family-owned and/or managed. This finding has already been discussed by Savage.[8] It means that these firms have been able to attain the size investigated largely through the proper selection of a growth segment. When the founder or family is unable to sustain that growth new activities have to be found which require investments possible beyond the potential of family funds and the company has to go public.[9] Diversification and the management of diversity is then handed to professionals.

> Family-managed firms control with more detail, more frequency and with less formalism than professionally managed firms (significant at $p < .05$ in all three countries).

An illustration is provided by the case of a firm with $200 million in sales and an annual growth rate of 25 per cent today which ten years ago had sales of only $21 million. It is a 1,000-person firm, yet is still entirely in the hands of the founder.

As the evidence suggests, such a firm was not likely to have a cost accounting and/or budgetary system in operation. Even if such systems had been put into effect during the last ten years they are not likely to cover many relevant aspects today. Here the emphasis and priority of top management are likely to be much less on modern control — which would leave him free from details (e.g. use of exception principles) — than on sustaining the growth. To give an example, one of the firms in the sample, a French electrical equipment firm, started in the 1950s and now employing more than 11,000 people. The top priority has not been modern control: the founder hired a controller for the first time two years ago. The priority has been geographic diversification and expansion of production units to cover the demand.

Besides the consequences of high growth in these firms on control, one could also argue that the power base of the owner-manager is his share of the capital of the firm whereas the professional manager's power is much more 'expert power'.[10] As a consequence formality in systems is not so necessary for the former, all the more so in that formalism may prevent him from stepping into operations whenever he likes and bypassing the heirarchy.

High-growth companies have often been equated in the literature with entrepreneurship.[11] The characteristics of the entrepreneur[12] make him feel more comfortable with informal and charismatic types of leadership than with formal systems. To him, control means reporting and surveillance more than guiding as witnessed in Germany where *Kontrolle* is associated with family management while 'controlling' was associated with professional management.

These remarks raise questions as to the *transition* needs of such companies in order to avoid the void created by such personalities who did not put into effect formal systems on which the organisation could rely in their absence.

4. INFLUENCE OF TECHNOLOGY AND MARKET STABILITY
(sectorial differences)

Two main propositions seem to be suggested by the data.

The effect of sector differences on top management control seems weak but more significant on operational control.

The primary difference at operating levels is that the more complex technology is and the more unstable the market environment is the less formal control is.

The first proposition runs somewhat against the contingency theory of management[13] which maintains that the basic management design is dependent upon the environment of a firm. Top management tasks seem to be independent of the sector they are in, whereas operational management is not. This apparent contradiction is in fact understandable. Most contingency theory proponents have investigated operational management. Lawrence and Lorsch's study of the impact of market environment on structure dealt mainly with differentiation and integration between the marketing departments, the research departments and the production departments of selected firms but not with top management tasks.[14] The studies by Pugh et al.,[15] Woodward[16] and Blauner[17] on the impact of technology on 'alienation' also dealt with operations or even workers.

Thus an area to be researched is whether top management tasks should also be viewed as contingent upon the sectors they are in. At least in practice, when new top management is called in, they seem to be hired more from successful companies than from companies in the same sector.

The second proposition, suggested and supported in the work of Child[18] and Perrow,[19] asserts that when there is a high variability in the environment (market and technology) a freer form of management is required to perform well. Electronics is representative of the sector in which variability is higher and textiles of one where it is lower.

Electronics firms are characterised by their relatively recent emergence on the business scene whereas textiles is a much older industry. Thus, more modern management techniques have been put into use in the former.

The profile of personnel at different levels in the hierarchy is different. Electronics firms need more trained and more skilled people at managerial as well as at supervisory levels: this in turn leads to more autonomy in control for people who are in a better position to take responsibility. Thus less formalism and frequency of control is needed.

Production control at the cost and manpower level is less important in electronics than in textiles: higher pay means higher stability of personnel. A focus on long-term market innovation and research is more crucial to success in electronics than on keeping short-run variable and fixed costs low, which is required in textiles, a labour-intensive activity.

5. THE LACK OF INFLUENCE OF STRATEGY ON CONTROL AND THE WEAK LINK WITH MANAGEMENT PROCESSES

There is not much evidence of a direct relationship between strategy and control. This may have to do with the lack of strategic control witnessed in the firms selected. Chief executives seemed to pay much more attention to internal routine short-term information (sales, deliveries) rather than focus their attention on critical factors for success or competitive strengths. Strategy, measured by diversification, was also not as strongly associated overall with structure and decentralisation of decision-making as found by the Harvard team of Bruce Scott.[20]

It may be due to the size of the firms selected. They are not in the top one hundred; they are thus less sophisticated and overall may not have the managerial skill needed in order to adopt the divisionalised structure. However, the mere fact that the companies selected are smaller than the ones usually investigated is a better representation of the economic and managerial level achieved in the three countries. (The top one hundred are more disposed to imitate international managerial skills which circulate in Western countries.) Thus, although authors have found a positive relationship between diversification and structure[21] when studying the first one hundred companies, in Great Britain, France and Germany, this study did not find as clear a relationship in smaller companies. The first proposition derived can be stated as follows:

Models of strategy-structure which apply to the largest companies do not apply as much to smaller companies.

An analysis by country shows that in Great Britain exceptions to this proposition exist; in fact, a significant positive correlation exists between diversification and structure. As noted in Chapter 4, and reinforced by the statistical analysis in France and Germany the adoption of the divisional structure was more a matter of philosophy and a willingness to decentralise than a matter of diversification. In these two countries — and especially in France — even for the top one hundred Dyas[22] has noted that the move to divisional structure and decentralisation in decision-making when the firm has become more diversified has been resisted by top management and as a result has taken longer than in the US. Moreover, both countries are categorised[23] as believing less in the individual capacity for initiative and leadership and as a result are less willing to decentralise. These data would suggest the following corresponding proposition:

Diversification will more often lead to multi-divisional

structure, decentralisation and thus less detail and centralism in control in Great Britain and other countries where authoritarian attitudes are less prevalent than in Germany, France or countries where authoritarian attitudes are more common.

The propositions covered in subsections 1 to 5 of this section suggest hypotheses for more directed research. The strong indication of multiple influences, however, should make future researchers wary of too narrow a focus.

SUGGESTIONS FOR RELATED RESEARCH

In its design the research presented has limited itself to Western advanced countries. In its coverage, it has focused on management control in a cybernetic view, thus not dealing with the relationship between control and behaviour. Finally, it has only touched on effectiveness. This would suggest three areas for further research.

THE CASE OF LESS DEVELOPED COUNTRIES

These countries are often characterised by a lack of managerial skills and the presence of either large international or nationalised groups together with family-dominated smaller firms. For the latter, this study would suggest that most of the behaviour witnessed in family-managed firms would prevail: less formalism, more autocratic styles and with control used more as a policing instrument than a guiding instrument. Also, the move from *Kontrolle* to 'controlling' in Germany would suggest that some sort of control would be necessary in those countries before planning starts.

In addition the companies investigated often had to bring in external managerial skills, often trained in subsidiaries of US firms or multinational companies, in order to reach the level of 'controlling'. The role of the multinational companies in bringing such skills to underdeveloped countries could be even larger. Many companies who have made the move to divisional structures in Germany or France have also brought in management consultants, mainly US ones.[24] For less-developed countries, the impact of such firms on managerial change could also be larger. Thus, four areas could be investigated:

1. The role of multinational corporations in fostering managerial skills in less-developed countries.
2. The role of management consultants in the same area.
3. The necessity, in comparative research dealing with less-developed countries, of separating family-owned enterprises in the analysis. In fact, in many comparative management designs comparisons are made between subsidiaries of US companies with local companies.[25] These local companies, however, may not be comparable to such subsidiaries as they are not professionally managed.
4. The need for control instruments in less-developed countries before being able to develop planning activities.

THE LINK OF MANAGEMENT CONTROL WITH LEADERSHIP AND MOTIVATION

This research has focused on management control in a cybernetic view, thus not dealing with the link between control and behavioral responses of people and their motivation. Evidence suggests that in all three countries control is not viewed as being related to motivation. However, management theory clearly states that in its differences phases — standard setting, measurement, evaluation — control needs positive behavioral responses of people in order to be effective.[26] For instance, Cammann and Nadler have noted the dysfunctions which can be created in measurement when people focus their attention on what is measured to look good.[27] Moreover, as eventually standards become objectives for employees, there is an assumption that if they are not met, something will happen in terms of rewards and/or punishments. This does not, however, seem to be very much the case in Europe. If results are not up to plans, there does not seem to be much of a link with rewards and/or sanctions which would make people adopt certain behaviours. However, this evidence is limited as behavioral responses of people to control were not directly assessed nor were the bases for rewards and punishments. Researchers in this area, however, should be wary of the fact that formal control systems may not be used so much in Europe as motivation devices as may be the case in the US.

CONTROL EFFECTIVENESS

One of the aims of comparative management study is to find ingredients for both macro and micro economic effectiveness.

In practice, the measurement of managerial effectiveness and efficiency is very difficult. The present study found the same difficulty. An attempt was made to obtain from senior managers data that would reveal the 'success' of the control practices being utilised, but it failed to uncover useful evaluative data. Even the costs of control were hard to isolate, and very few of the managers interviewed were able to separate the effect of their managerial activities from the influences of external economic influences.

So control effectiveness remains an important but uncharted area for research. What specific factors lead to effectiveness on a company basis? Is it the quality of information supplied? Is it the speed of information? Does it have to do with participation in standards setting, or with the positive responses of people, or with the efforts devoted to control? Is it related to the internal coherence of control with other management processes such as leadership and structure?

These areas have often been proposed as determinants of control success and should be included in such studies.

The present study contributes to future research on control effectiveness. The elements of control and the main factors which influence the design of control systems have been identified: the model presented earlier in this chapter provides a framework for understanding why controls in a particular company take the form they do. This could be a starting point for analysing control targets and for explaining success or failure. In view of the country differences the present study found, the effectiveness and efficiency of control is likely to vary among countries.

SUMMARY

The relative impact of country, business (sector and strategy), management system (structure and planning) variables, as well as professionalism, on selected characteristics of control has been assessed. It has permitted us to draw a general model of control practices across countries. From this model, general propositions have been explicated which shed some light on the interactions between control, country and management theory variables. These propositions show that country is not the sole factor to influence control practices. Thus the culture-bound school of comparative management is challenged: further research will need to bring in management principles if one wants to avoid a black-box approach in comparative studies. Universal principles seem in fact to apply more when one looks at the direction of changes from one system to another, whereas country factors seem to play a larger role when one looks at the level of practices. As such this exploratory study will hopefully permit more directed research on management phenomena across countries.

NOTES

1. W. H. Newman and E. K. Warren, *The Process of Management*, 4th edn. (Englewoods Cliffs, N.J.: Prentice Hall, 1977) p. 511.
2. W. H. Newman and E. K. Warren, op. cit., p. 517–18.
3. R. P. Rumelt, *Strategy, Structure and Economic Performance in Large American Industrial Corporations* (Boston: Harvard University Press, 1974).
4. Theodore D. Weinschall, 'Multinational Corporations – Their Development and Universal Role', *Management International Review*, vol. 15, no. 2 (1975); 'Multinational Corporations – Their Study and Measurement', *Management International Review*, vol. 15, no. 3 (1975).
5. W. H. Newman and E. K. Warren, op. cit., ch. 29.
6. J. W. Lorsch and S. A. Allen, *Managing Diversity and Interdependence* (Boston: Harvard Graduate School of Business Administration, 1973).
7. W. H. Newman and E. K. Warren, op. cit., p. 460; J. H. Horovitz and D. Xardel, *Diriger Une Entreprise Moyenne* (Paris: Les Editions d'Organisation, 1977), ch. 7.
8. D. Savage, 'Les Dirigeants et la Croissance de l'Entreprise', *Sociologie du Travail*, vol. 2 (April–June 1975) pp. 136–51.
9. Witnessed in D. F. Channon, *The Strategy and Structure of British Enterprises* (London: Macmillan, 1973) Table 3–5, p. 76.
10. J. R. P. French and B. Raven, 'The Bases of Social Power', in D. Cartwright and A. Zander (eds.), *Group Dynamics*, 3rd edn (New York: Harper and Row, Publishers, 1968) pp. 259–69, discusses different bases for power.
11. D. Savage, op. cit.
12. J. Laufer 'Comment Devient-on Entrepreneur?' *Revue Francaise de Gestion*, vol. 2 (1976).

13. R. H. Hall, *Organizations: Structures and Processes* (Englewoods Cliffs, N.J.: Prentice Hall, 1972), ch. 10.
14. P. R. Lawrence and Jay W. Lorsch, *Organization and Environment: Managing Differentiation and Integration* (Cambridge, Mass.: Harvard Graduate School of Business Administration, 1967).
15. D. S. Pugh, D. J. Hickson, C. R. Hinings and C. Turner, 'The Context of Organization Structure', *Administrative Science Quarterly*, vol. 14, no. 1 (March 1969).
16. Joan Woodward, *Industrial Organizations* (London: Oxford University Press, 1962).
17. R. Blauner, *Alienation and Freedom* (Chicago: University of Chicago Press, 1964).
18. J. Child, 'Managerial and Organizational Factors Associated with Company Performance; Part II, A Contingency Analysis', *Journal of Management Studies*, vol. 12 (1973), pp. 12–27.
19. C. Perrow, *Organizational Analysis: A Sociological Perspective* (Belmont, Calif.: Wadsworth Publishing Co., 1970).
20. The team studied the relationship between Strategy and Structure in France, Great Britain and Germany for the top hundred companies. See D. F. Channon, op. cit., for Great Britain; G. P. Dyas and H. T. Thanheiser, The Emerging European Enterprise (London: Macmillan Press Ltd, 1973), for France and Germany.
21. Although in their study they concentrated on structural divisions of labour (functional versus divisionalised structures), these authors generalised their references to all management processes (i.e., planning, control and decentralisation of decision-making).
22. G. P. Dyas and H. T. Thanheiser, op. cit., p. 240.
23. M. Haire, E. E. Ghiselli, L. W. Porter, *Managerial Thinking: an International Study* (New York: John Wiley and Sons, 1966).
24. Noted both in D. F. Channon, op. cit., and in G. Dyas and H. T. Thanheiser, op. cit.
25. A. R. Negandhi and B. D. Estafen, 'A Research Model to Determine the Applicability of American Know-How in Different Cultures and/or Environments', *Academy of Management Journal*, vol. 8, no. 4 (December 1965).
26. W. H. Newman, E. K. Warren, op. cit., ch. 23.
27. C. Cammann and D. A. Nadler, 'Fit Control Systems to Your Managerial Style', *Harvard Business Review* (January–February 1976) pp. 65–72.
28. W. H. Newman, E. K. Warren, op. cit., ch. 23.

Conclusion: Some Implications for Managers[1]

Implications for managers must be regarded with caution owing to the exploratory nature of our in-depth study. It seems, however, that each country can borrow from the other within its own philosophy, within its constraints, not only for local managers but also for multinational managers.

Of course the solution to each company's preoccupation is different, depending on where it stands as compared to current practices. Nevertheless, the most striking observation is that managers in France, Great Britain and Germany are not learning much from each other. At least with respect to managerial control, strengths are coupled with weaknesses. No company in our sample of not-so-large indigenous concerns is taking full advantage of the potential combination of skills. So let us look briefly at each country – its characteristic strengths and its opportunity of learning from its neighbours.

BRITISH MANAGEMENT

British firms seem well-equipped for financial control and are doing a good job here. Measures of objectives as well as performance are not mixed with fiscal accounting, and control

---

1. This chapter is a partial reproduction of an article published by the author in: 'Management Control in France, Great Britain, Germany', *Columbia Journal of World Business* (Summer 1978), pp. 16–22, with permission.

bears not only on the attainment of profit and cash flow targets but also comprehends the management of assets and especially cash, an important item in an inflationary economy. In addition, forward-rolling forecasts and highlights of main results provide managers with a guiding instrument. Long-range planning has been going on now for several years; and managers are stimulated through the planning process to think ahead, to make predictions so as to be able to correct decisions, if required. Manuals and procedures are quite impressive and advanced, and provide ample opportunities for line management to think in terms of the best allocation of resources. In marketing control, processes seem adequately decentralised to allow the responsible person to monitor performance and take whatever steps are necessary to reach formulated goals.

On the other hand, British managers can learn something from the Germans about control of production With engineering precision and disciplined management of operating conditions, the Germans plan and then control activities clear down to well-defined cost centres as small as a dozen workers. Moreover, they often establish management by projects which are an explicit step in a long-range plan. This kind of planning and control forces managers to determine key efficiency objectives, key tasks, key responsibilities and key dates; it can be a vital tool for closing the gap between actual performance and strictly financial plans.

Of course, the British managers neither can, will, nor should take over German production controls in toto. Major adjustments such as the following would be necessary. (1) The detailed planning and exercise of control can be done within each subsidiary – not centralised as in Germany. Nevertheless, group managers will have to take a much more active role in designing and monitoring the localised systems. Control via financial results alone – now typical of British firms – is too remote and indirect. (2) The manner of setting standards and requesting corrective action will have to be suited to local social relationships. Firmness and openness can go together.

In addition, British senior managers can relate their controlling more effectively to strategic moves in the following ways:

1. Close the gap between long-range strategic plans and short-run efficient financial plans by one-year programming

and project management, especially in the area of production.
2. Emphasise more strategic control at the top managerial level, in order to evaluate a subsidiary not only by its cash and income statement, but also in terms of its long-term development. This may require less financial information but the development or *key indicators* for each area (or activity) which can help both at the planning stage (e.g. probe the strategies presented by each activity) and at the monitoring stage.

GERMAN MANAGEMENT

The main strengths of the German control system which may be inferred from the research are its orientation towards short-term operational efficiency – especially in production – and its ability to work on and monitor projects dealing with such efficiency. As already noted, these controls are very effective.

The typical German production control, however, does require a large central staff with a great mass of detailed data flowing into central headquarters. Past emphasis had been on close surveillance. A constructive shift is occurring in some, though not all, German companies from the old style '*Kontrolle*' to a new emphasis on 'Control'. The new pattern focuses attention on key figures and selectively highlights key problems; more emphasis is given to guidance rather than past performance. An aspect of this shift is – like the British planners – a separation of control from financial record-keeping.

The main potential British contributions to German control systems involve (1) greater flexibility especially in dealing with intractable marketing problems, and (2) more attention to strategic moves. The British achieve these ends primarily through decentralisation of planning, and also through a laxness in control itself – neither of which means it fits easily into the German management philosophy. Nevertheless, other ways of achieving similar ends can be devised. The following suggestions move in this direction.

1. Separate management control from accounting. Although the computer is handy for providing information on both,

it is not required to handle management control in such a way, as the British case shows. Separating the two might allow a focus on information which is more important for decision-making as opposed to recording.
2. Put more emphasis on strategic planning and strategic control especially in those areas where international markets are becoming more competitive. In this area, separating the long-range planning process from the budgets and control department may be required.
3. Give more flexibility in the marketing area by specifying control characteristics which are different from production. Discipline, cost consciousness and short-term results may be in order in production, but marketing cannot be reduced to such quantitative measures.

FRENCH MANAGEMENT

In France, a modern minority of firms have controls which tend to follow the German pattern but with some British features in the financial area. These companies are seeking a balance between German 'tightness' and British 'flexibility'. As yet no clear reconciliation has emerged, partly because the typical French form of organisation differs so widely from the British decentralised 'holding' structure.

For a large majority of French firms, however, the problem lies not so much in control as in planning. Without adequate planning, control becomes a rather diffuse task: it is a mixture of accounting, fiscal income statement surveillance and informal power exercised by the chief executive. The lack of system is even more pronounced when companies are headed by the founder or held by a family. As long as the chief executive, through his personality, charismatic role and sense of direction, can stay on top of things, especially in high-growth markets, a company can develop without much formal planning and control. Trouble arises when growth slows down and especially when the key executive drops out of the picture. The options then are either failure or professional management.

This study provides some idealistic suggestions for such a newly appointed professional manager of a French company. For financial and marketing planning and control, draw on

Conclusion: Some Implications for Managers

British practice; for production planning and control, turn to the newer German design centring on 'control'; and for strategic planning and control, look to proposals for improving both designs (reflecting advanced US practice). The obvious drawback of such a composite is that we found no organisation model which provides the necessary support for the combined set of controls.

In current practice, for companies of the size and nature covered in this study, French organisation is much closer to the German pattern than the British pattern — functional departments and centralised; and current economic and social pressures in France push towards continuing centralisation. Consequently, when the newly appointed professional manager takes over he probably should look to the German pattern of control — but modified in the manner recommended above.

IMPLICATIONS FOR MULTINATIONAL CORPORATIONS

Besides country-specific directions for improvement, this research study provides some implications for multinational corporations. The results tend to show that standard universal management principles should be applied differently in each country depending on the key characteristics of the planning structure and general management style which predominate in that particular country. By 'applied differently' we mean that before standardising the foreign affiliate's management design to meet headquarter's wishes in the control area, careful assessment should be made of the way local variables impact on the structure of planning and control. If there is quite a difference from the customary structure in the headquarter's country, then leads and lags in management sophistication should be recognised. For instance, acquiring a subsidiary in France may require training in marketing control and a longer time for people to learn how to decentralise and use planning than would be necessary in Great Britain. Examples of the local factors that should be assessed include:

1. The impact of current educational backgrounds on control emphasis: training may be needed in weak areas (production control in Great Britain, marketing control in France, for instance).

2. The impact of beliefs and attitudes towards authority and centralism: more time and effort may be required to decentralise in country with strong habits of centralisation.
3. The levels of sophistication in planning achieved: to fit headquarter's needs, more training might be needed in that area to arrive at adequate control.

At least by being aware of such variations, mistakes may be avoided in pushing too many new control mechanisms.

Comparative in-depth studies of managerial practices in additional countries will, of course, provide more insights on 'what works well where'. The findings of the three-country study reported here were sufficiently rich to enthusiastically recommend that such studies be made.

Bibliography

Ackoff, R. L. *A Concept of Corporate Planning* (New York: John Wiley and Sons, 1970).
Ajiferuke, M. and Boddewyn, J. 'Culture and Other Explanatory Variables in Comparative Management Studies.' *Academy of Management Journal*, vol. 8, no. 2 (June 1970).
Alsegg, R. J. 'Control Relationships between American Corporations and their European Subsidiaries.' American Management Association, Research Study, no. 107 (1971).
Argyris, C., *Integrating the Individual and the Organization* (New York: John Wiley and Sons, 1964).
Barrett, G. V. and Bass, B. R. 'Comparative Surveys of Managerial Attitudes and Behavior.' in J. Boddewyn (ed.), *Comparative Management, Teaching, Training, Research* (New York: New York University Press, 1970).
Blauner, R. *Alienation and Freedom* (Chicago: University of Chicago Press, 1964).
Blough, R. *International Business: Environment and Adaptation* (New York: McGraw-Hill, 1966).
Boddewyn, J. *Comparative Management and Marketing* (Glenview, Ill.: Scott, Foresman and Co., 1969).
— — *Comparative Management, Teaching, Training, Research* (New York: New York University Press, 1970).
Bourricaud, François. 'Sociologie du Chef d'Entreprise: Le Jeune Patron.' *Revue Economique*, vol. 6 (November 1958).
Brandt, W. K. and Hulbert, J. M. 'Patterns of Communications in the Multinational Corporation: an Empirical Study.' Research Paper no. 76. New York: Graduate School of Business, Columbia University, 1974.
— —. For instance, 'Marketing Strategies of American European and Japanese Multinational Subsidiaries.' Paper presented at the Academy of International Business Meetings, Fontainebleau, France (7–9 July 1975).
Brooke, M. Z. and Rammers, H. L. *The Strategy of Multinational Enterprise* (London: Longman Group, 1970).
Burns, T. and Stalker, G. M. *The Management of Innovation*, 2nd edn (Tavistock Publications, 1962).
Cammann, C. and Nadler, D. A. 'Fit Control Systems to your Managerial Style.' *Harvard Business Review* (January–February 1976).

Chandler, A. D. *Strategy and Structure* (Cambridge, Mass.: MIT Press, 1962).
Channon, D. F. *The Strategy and Structure of British Enterprise* (London: Macmillan, 1973).
Child, J. 'Managerial and Organizational Factors Associated with Company Performance: Part II, A Contingency Analysis.' *Journal of Management Studies* (1973).
Clark, A. W. and McCabe S. 'Leadership Beliefs of Australian Managers', in W. K. Graham, K. H. Roberts (eds.), *Comparative Studies in Organizational Behavior* (New York: Holt, Rinehart and Winston, 1972).
Crozier, Michel. *The Bureaucratic Phenomenon* (Chicago: University of Chicago Press, 1964).
Cyert, R. M. and March J. G. *A Behavioral Theory of the Firm* (Englewood Cliffs, N.J.: Prentice-Hall, 1963).
Dalton, G. W. and Lawrence, P. R. *Motivation and Control in Organizations* (Homewood, Ill.: Richard D. Irwin and the Dorsey Press, 1971).
Davis, S. 'US vs Latin America Business and Culture.' *Harvard Business Review* (November 1969).
Douglass, M. E. 'Testing a Methodology for Measuring the Interaction between Organization and Environment.' *Management International Review*, vol. 15, no. 1 (1975).
Dubin, R., 'Supervision and Productivity: Empirical Findings and Theoretical Considerations', in R. Dubin, G. Homans, F. Mann and D. Miller, *Leadership and Productivity* (Calif.: Chandler Publishing, 1965).
Duncan, R. B. 'Characteristics of Organization Environment.' *Administrative Science Quarterly*, vol. 17, no. 3 (September 1972).
Dyas, G. P. and Thanheiser, H. T. *The Emerging European Entreprise.* (London: Macmillan, 1976).
Estafen, B. D. 'Methods for Management Research in the 1970s: An Ecological System Approach.' *Academy of Management Journal* (March 1971).
—— 'The Systems Transfer Characteristics of Firms in Spain: a Comparative Management Study.' Indiana University, Graduate School of Business, International Research Series, no. 5.
—— 'An Empirical Experiment in Comparative Management: a Study of the Transferability of American Management Policies and Practices into Firms Operating in Chile.' Ph.D. Dissertation, UCLA, Graduate School of Business, 1967.
Evers, Heinrich. *Kriterien Zur Auslese von Top Managern in Großunternehmen: Eine Empirische Untersuchung* (Frankfurt/M.: Harri Deutsch, 1974).
Farmer, R. N. and Richman B. M. 'A Model for Research in Comparative Management.' *California Management Review*, vol. 2, no. 2. (Winter 1964).
—— *International Business: an Operational Theory* (Homewood, Ill.: Richard D. Irwin, 1966).
—— *Comparative Management and Economic Progress* (Homewood, Ill.: Richard D. Irwin, 1965).

—— 'A Model for Research in Comparative Management.' *California Management Review*, vol. 7 (Winter 1964).
Farris, G. F. and Butterfield, D. A. 'Control Theory in Brazilian Organizations.' *Administrative Science Quarterly*, vol. 17. (1972).
Fayerweather. *The Executive Overseas* (New York: Syracuse University Press, 1959).
Fayol, H. *General and Industrial Management* (London: Pitman, 1949).
French, J. R. P. and Raven, B. 'The Bases of Social Power' in D. Cartwright and A. Zander (eds.), *Group Dynamics*, 3rd edn (New York: Harper and Row, 1968).
Gabriel. *The International Transfer of Corporate Skills: Management Contacts in Less Different Countries* (Cambridge, Mass.: Harvard Business School, Division of Research, 1967).
Galbraith, J. K. *The New Industrial State* (New York: Signet Books, 1968).
Gonzales, R. F. and McMillan, C. 'The Universality of American Management Philosophy.' *Academy of Management Journal*, vol. 4, no. 1 (1961).
Granick, D. *The European Executive* (New York: Doubleday and Co., 1962).
—— *Managerial Comparisons of Four Developed Countries: France, Great Britain, United States and Russia* (Cambridge, Mass.: MIT Press, 1972).
Greiner, L. A. 'Evolutions and Revolutions as Organizations Grow.' *Harvard Business Review* (July–August 1972).
Grosset, S. *Management, European and American Styles* (Belmont, Calif.: Wadsworth Publishing Co., 1970).
Gulick, L. and Urwick, L. F. (eds.), *Papers on the Science of Administration* (New York: Columbia University, Institute of Public Administration, 1937).
Gussman, B. *Out in the Midday Sun* (New York: Oxford University Press, 1963).
Guth, W. D. and Tagiuri, R. 'Personal Values and Corporate Strategy.' *Harvard Business Review* (May–June 1965).
Haire, M., Ghiselli, E. E. and Porter, L. W. *Managerial Thinking, an International Study* (New York: John Wiley and Sons, 1966).
Hall, R. H. *Organizations: Structures and Processes* (Englewood Cliffs, N.J.: Prentice-Hall, 1972).
Harbison, F. H. and Myers, C. A. *Management in the Industrial World* (New York: McGraw-Hill, 1959).
Hartmann, H. *Authority and Organization in German Management* (Princeton, N.J.: Princeton University Press, 1959).
Henzler, Herbert. 'Angriff Auf Ein Tabu.' art. n.p. (April 1975).
—— 'Der Januskopf muss weg!' *Wirtschaftwoche*, no. 38 (13 September 1974).
Herzberg, F., Mausner, B. and Snyderman, B. *The Motivation to Work* (New York: John Wiley and Sons, 1959).
Hesserling, Pjotr. 'Studies in Cross-Cultural Organization.' *Columbia Journal of World Business* (December 1973).

Hoffmann, F. *Entwicklung der Organizations Forschung Zur Verarberte und Erweiterte Aufgabe* (Wiesbaden, 1976).
—— 'Der Controller in Deutschen Industriebetrieb.' *Der Betrieb*, no. 21 (December 1968).
Horovitz, J. H. and Xardel, D. *Diriger une Entreprise Moyenne* (Paris: Les Editions d'Organisation, 1977).
Ivens, M. 'Behind the Organization Man.' *Twentieth Century*, vol. 17, no. 3 (Spring 1965).
Kavcic, B., Rus, V. and Tannenbaum, A. S. 'Control, Participation and Effectiveness in Four Industrial Organization.' *Administrative Science Quarterly* (March 1971).
Koontz, H. 'A Model for Analysing the Universality and Transferability of Management.' *Academy of Management Journal*, vol. 12, no. 4 (December 1969).
Krantz, A. I. IBM, 'Some Recent Advances in Cross-National Management Research.' *Academy of Management Journal*, vol. 18, no. 3 (1975).
Laufer, J. 'Comment devient-on Entrepreneur?' *Revue Francaise de Gestion*, vol. 2 (1976).
Lauter, G. P. 'Environment Constraints Impeding Managerial Performance in Developing Countries.' *Management International Review*, 10-2-3 (1970).
Lauterback, A. *Enterprise in Latin America* (Ithaca: Cornell University Press, 1966).
Lawrence, P. R. and Lorsch, J. W. *Organization and Environment* (Cambridge, Mass.: Harvard Business School, Division of Research, 1967).
—— *Organization and Environment: Managing Differentiation and Integration* (Cambridge, Mass.: Harvard Graduate School of Business Administration, 1967).
Learned, E. P., Christensen, C. R., Andrews, K. R., Guth, W. D. *Business Policy Text and Cases* (Homewood, Ill.: Richard D. Irwin, 1969).
Likert, R. *New Patterns of Management*. New York: McGraw-Hill, 1961.
Lindblom, C. E. 'The Science of Muddling Through.' *Public Administration Review*, vol. 19, no. 2 (1959).
Lorsch, J. W. and Allen, S. A. *Managing Diversity and Interdependence*. Boston: Harvard Graduate School of Business Administration, 1973.
McClelland and Winter, *Motivating Economic Achievement* (New York: Free Press, 1969).
McMahon, J. T. and Ivancevich, J. M. 'A Study of Control in a Manufacturing Organization, Managers and Non Managers.' *Administrative Science Quarterly*, vol. 21 (1976).
Mouton and Blake. 'Issues in Transnational Organization Development', in B. M. Bass, R. C. Cooper and J. A. Haas (eds.), *Managing for Accomplishment* (Lexington, Mass.: Heath Lexington, 1970).
Nath, R. 'A Methodological Review of Cross Cultural Management Research.' *International Social Science Journal* (Spring 1968).
—— 'A Methodological Review of Cross-Cultural Management Research' in J. Boddewyn (ed.), *Comparative Management and Marketing* (Glenview, Ill.: Scott, Foresman, 1969).
Negandhi, A. R. 'A Model for Analysing Organizations in Cross-Cultural

Settings: A Conceptual Scheme and Some Research Findings', in Comparative Administration and Management Conference, Bureau of Economic and Business Research (Ohio: Kent State University, 1968).
Negandhi, A. R. and Estafen, B. D. 'A Research Model to Determine the Applicability of American Know-How in Different Cultures and/or Environments.' *Academy of Management Journal*, vol. 8, no. 4 (December 1965).
—— 'American Management Abroad: A Comparative Study of Management Practices of American Subsidiaries and Local Firms in Developing Countries.' *Management International Review*, 11-4-5 (1971).
—— 'Cross-Cultural Management Studies: too many Conclusions not enough Conceptualization.' *Management International Review* (1974).
Negandhi, A. R. and Prasad, S. B. *Comparative Management*. New York: Appleton-Century Crofts, 1970.
—— 'Comparative Management and Organization Theory: a Marriage Needed.' *Academy of Management Journal*, vol. 18, no. 2 (June 1975).
Newman, W. H. *Constructive Control* (Englewood Cliffs, N.J.: Prentice-Hall, 1975).
—— and Logan, J. P. *Strategy, Policy and Central Management*, 6th edn (South Western Publishing, 1971).
——, Summer, C. E. and Warren, E. K. *The Process of Management*, 3rd edn (Englewood Cliffs, N.J.: Prentice-Hall, 1972).
—— and Warren, E. K. *The Process of Management*, 4th edn. Englewood Cliffs, N.J.: Prentice-Hall, 1977.
Nowothny. 'American vs European Management Philosophy.' *Harvard Business Review* (March—April, 1964).
Oberg, W. 'Cross-Cultural Perspectives on Management Principles.' *Academy of Management Journal*, vol. 6, no 2 (June 1963).
Perlmutter, H. U. 'L'Entreprise Internationale. Trois Conceptions.' *Revue Economique et Sociale*, vol. 23, no. 2 (May 1965).
Perrow, C. *Organizational Analysis: a Sociological View* (Belmont, Calif.: Wadsworth Publishing, 1970).
—— *Organizational Analysis: A Sociological Perspective* (Belmont, Calif.: Wadsworth Publishing, 1970).
Philipps, ?. and Slocum, J. W. Jr. 'A Comparative Study of American and Mexican Operatives.' *Academy of Management Journal*, vol. 14, no. 1 (March 1971).
Pitts, J. R. 'The Bourgeois Family and French Economic Retardation.' PhD. Dissertation (Cambridge, Mass.: Harvard University, 1957).
Pugh, D. S., Hickson, D. J., Hinings, C. R. and Turner, C. 'The Context of Organization Structure.' *Administrative Science Quarterly*, vol. 14, no 1 (March 1969).
Richman, B. M. *Soviet Management: with Significant American Comparisons*. (Englewood Cliffs, N.J.: Prentice-Hall, 1965).
Roberts, K. H. 'On Looking at an Elephant: an Evaluation of Cross-Cultural Research Related to Organizations.' *Psychological Bulletin* (November 1970).
—— and Graham, W. K. (eds.), *Comparative Studies in Organizational Behavior* (New York: Holt, Rinehart and Winston, 1972).

Robock, S. H. and Simmonds, K. *International Business and Multinational Enterprises* (Homewood, Ill.: Richard D. Irwin, 1973).
Rostow, W. W. *The States of Economic Growth* (Cambridge, Mass.: Harvard University Press, 1962).
Rumelt, R. P. *Strategy, Structure and Economic Performance in Large American Industrial Corporations* (Boston: Harvard University Press, 1974).
Rutenberg, D. P. 'Organizational Archetypes of a Multinational Company.' *Management Science*, vol. 16, no. 6 (February 1970).
Savage, D. 'Les Dirigeants et al Croissance de l'Entreprise.' *Sociologie du Travail*, vol. 2 (April–June 1975).
Schollhammer, H. 'Strategies in Comparative Management Theorizing', in J. Boddewyn (ed.), *Comparative Management Proceedings* (New York: New York University, Graduate School of Business, 1970).
— — 'Strategies and Methodologies in International Business and Comparative Management.' *Management International Review* (1973).
— — 'The Comparative Management Theory Jungle.' *Academy of Management Journal*, vol. 12, no. 1 (March 1969).
Scott, B. R. 'The Stages of Corporate Development.' *Business Policy Notes 998,999* (Boston: Harvard University, Graduate School of Business Administration, 1971).
— — 'The Industrial State: Old Myths and New Realities.' *Harvard Business Review* (March–April 1973).
Sehti, S. P. and Curry, D. 'Variable and Object Clustering of Cross-Cultural Data: some Implications for Comparative Research and Policy Formulation', in S. P. Sehti, and J. N. Sheth, *Multinational Business Operations, Long-Range Planning, Organisation and Management* (Calif.: Goodyear Publishing Co., 1973).
Sherman. *It All Depends* (New York: American Management Association, 1970).
Sirota, D. and Greenwood, J. M. 'Understand Your Overseas Work Force.' *Harvard Business Review*, vol. 49, no. 1 (1971)
— — 'International Survey of Job Goals and Beliefs.' Paper presented at the 16th International Congress of Applied Psychology. Amsterdam, 1968.
Stahl, W. *Der Elitereislauf in der Unternehmerschaft* (Frankfurt/M.: Harri Deutsch, 1973).
Steiner, G. A. *Top Management Planning* (New York: Macmillan Company, 1969).
Stopford, J. and Wells, L. T. *Managing the Multinational Enterprise* (New York: Basic Books, 1972).
Tannenbaum, A. S. and Zupanov, J. 'The Distribution of Control in Some Yugoslav Industrial Organizations as Perceived by Members', in A. S. Tannenbaum (ed.), *Control in Organizations* (New York: McGraw-Hill, 1968).
— — 'Control in Organizations: Individual Adjustment and Organizational Performance.' *Administrative Science Quarterly* vol. 2 (1962).
Taylor, F. W. *Principles of Scientific Management* (New York: Harper and Row, 1911).

Thiagaragan and Bass. 'Differential Preferences or Long- vs short-term pay-offs in India and the United States.' *Proceedings 16th Annual Congress of Applied Psychology* (Amsterdam: Swets & Zeitlinger, 1969).

Trepo, G. X. 'The Introduction of Management by Objectives in France — Reality or Ritual?' Doctoral Thesis, Harvard Business School, 1971.

Vernon, R. *Sovereignty at Bay, the Multinational Spread of US Entreprises* (New York: Basic Books, 1971).

Wallich, H. C. *Mainsprings of the German Revival* (New Haven, Conn.: Yale University Press, 1955).

Warner and Abegglen. *Big Business Leaders in Latin America*.

Webber, R. A. *Management* (Homewood, Ill.: R. D. Irwin, 1975).

Weinschall, T. D. 'Communication, Culture and the Education of Multinational Managers', in T. D. Weinschall (ed.), *Culture and Management*, (Harmondsworth, Middx.: Penguin Books, 1977).

—— 'Multinational Corporations — Their Development and Universal Role.' *Management International Review*, vol. 15, no. 2 (1975).

Woodward, J. *Industrial Organizations* (London: Oxford University Press, 1962).

Wrapp, H. E. 'Good Managers Don't Make Policy Decisions.' *Harvard Business Review* (September–October 1967).

Wrigely, L. 'Divisional Autonomy and Diversification.' Doctoral Thesis, Harvard University (Boston: Graduate School of Business Administration, 1971).

Zenoff, D. B. and Zwick, J. *International Financial Management* (Englewood Cliffs, N.J.: Prentice-Hall, 1969).

Index

Ackoff, R. L., 9n19, 29, 36n9
Ajiferuke, M., 14n26, 17n49
Alsegg, R. J., 16n46
Anglo-Saxon, 15, 40, 152, 158
Argyris, C., 31, 36n13
Authoritarian, 154–5, 180

Barret, G. V. and Bass, B. R., 11, 15, 20n10, 21n33
Black box approach, 14
Blauner, R., 178, 184n17
Blough, R., 16, 22n45
Boddewyn, J., 10, 11, 19n4, 19n7
Bourricaud, F., 158n16
Brandt, W. K., 16, 22n47
Brooke, M. Z., 9n2
Budgets, 30, 77, 107, 120, 121, 122, 123, 159, 174, 188
Burns, T., 32, 37n21
Business variable, 162

Cammann, C., 181, 184n27, 122, 123
Capital expenditures, 121, 122, 123
Centralisation, 66, 122–4, 143 154–7, 189
Chandler, A. P., 32, 37n23
Channon, D. F., 58n4, 176n9 180n24
Chief executives, 74, 80, 84, 89, 90 92, 98, 101, 151, 152, 154, 157, 174–9, 188
Child, J., 178, 184n18
Clark, A. W., 11n19
cluster, 13, 152
    cultural, 39
Committee management, 67

Comparative management, 4, 17, 182
    black box approach to, 14, 183
    critical issues in, 10, 11
    individualistic approach to, 1
    objectives and scope of, 9, 18
    universal approach to, 1
Computers, 84, 99, 101, 113–14, 157
Control department, 105–7
Controllers, 71–2, 123–4, 157
    functions, 107, 110
    objectives, 106
Controlling, 71, 109, 110–12, 122, 153–5, 174–7, 180–6
Cost, 107–8, 112, 113, 115, 119, 124, 155–9, 174
    accounting, 109, 115–16, 125
    control, 112
    department, 115
    financial, 48
    personnel, 113–14
Critical issues, 11
Cross-cultural, 14, 34
Cross-national, 14, 18, 104
Crozier, M., 157n13
Cultural traits, 149, 151, 154, 157, 160
Cyert, R. M., 34n33

DAFSA, notice ser, 42
Dalton, G. W., 25n2
Data, 48, 72–6, 80, 93, 105, 150–4 162–4, 174, 177, 178, 182
    collection, 43
    on technology, 47
    process, 107
Davis, S., 16, 21n38

Debate between universal and
    cultural view, 170
Decentralisation, 34, 63–6, 96, 131,
    143–8, 152, 153, 159, 166–7,
    171, 178, 179, 180–8
Delegation of authority, 53–4, 66,
    119, 125, 159
Differences, 11, 14–18, 53–5,
    64–9, 71, 72, 74, 80, 82, 87,
    90–2, 104–5, 125, 148,
    160, 162, 166, 167, 177,
    181, 182, 189
Dimensions
    informal-formal, 28
    overall-detailed, 29
    time-span, 29
Diversification, 57, 59
Division, 54, 117
    of labour, 55, 179
Divisional structure, 59, 99, 117,
    148
    British, 59
    French, 63
    German, 62
Douglass, M. E., 14n36
Dubin, R., 32, 37n19
Ducan, P. B., 32n27
Dyas, G. P., 58n5, 179, 184n22

Economic conditions, 150, 151, 155
Education level, 149, 150, 156, 159
Empirical evidence, 14
Estafen, B. D., 14, 21n29
Evers, 35, 156n11
Exchange rates, 76
Explanation, 10–16, 93–8, 149,
    150, 154, 155, 156, 158,
    162, 167

Farmer, R. N., 13, 20n20, 35n35
Farris, G. F., 11, 13n51
Fashion, 27
Fayerweather, J., 12, 20n17
Fayol, H., 30, 36n10
Formalism, 79, 138, 143, 153, 156,
    158, 164–8, 176–8, 180
    in operational control, 129,
    163–7, 177
French, J. R., 177n10

Function, 79, 89, 104, 165
    of control department, 107
    the controllership, 105
Functional, 148, 170, 189
    approach, 76
    emphasis, 89
    organisation, 55–9, 117, 173

Gabriel, 193
Galbraith, J. K., 24n1
Generalisations, 15
Gonzales, R. F., 13, 20n23
Graham, W. K., 4
Granick, D., 16, 21n37
Greiner, L. A., 32, 37n24
Grosset, S., 155, 161n8
Gulick, L., 31, 36n12
Gussman, B., 16, 22n39
Guth, W. D., 34n1

Haire et. al., 13, 152, 160n4
Hall, R. H., 177n13
Harbison, F. H., 10, 19n3, 154, 161n7
Hartmann, H., 154n5, 155, 161n10
Headquarters, 56, 62, 108, 115, 120,
    137, 171–5, 187–9
Herbert, 109n1
Herzberg, F., 31n15
Hesserling, P., 17n48
Hoffmann, F., 45n14
Hopkins, J., 28
Horovitz, J. H. and Xardel, D., 175n7
Human resources, 107
Hyperspecialisation, 54

Implication, 149
    for managers, 185
    for miltinational corporation, 189
    for research, 17
Independent variables, 30
Indexes control, 164, 166
Industries
    choice of, 40
    criteria for choosing, 40
Inflation, 150–5
Information, 29, 69, 80, 83, 84, 86,
    93, 95, 96, 98, 105, 114, 115,
    117, 118, 124, 153, 155,
    158, 163–7, 175, 182,
    187, 188

Interview
  chief executive, 43
  guidelines, 47
  person, 43
  process, 47
Ivens, M., 150n1

Kavcic, B., 4
Kolmogorov-Smirnow, (test), 90
Kontrolle, 108–9, 111–12, 153, 174–7, 180–7
Koontz, H., 12, 20n15, 171
Krantz, A. I., 13n48
Kruskall-Wallis test, 82

Laufer, J., 177n12
Lauter, G. P., 16n36
Lauterbach, A., in Latin America, 16, 21n38
Lawrence, P. R., 32, 37, 178
Learned, E. P., 32, 37n25
Likert, R., 31, 36n14
Lindblom, C. E., 34n33
Long range planning, 70, 71, 72, 73, 77, 79, 107, 122–3, 153, 174, 186–8
  approach to, 75
Lorsch, J. W., 32, 37n 20 173n6–8

Macro-economic models, 17
Management by exception, 103
Managerial methods, 34
Marketing, 90, 92, 97, 121–2, 133–6, 154–9, 165
  control, 125, 131, 133, 138, 143, 144, 148, 149, 153, 186–9
  director, 49
  department, 137
  formalism, 130–8
  managers, 46, 133
  matters, 150
  objectives, 134–5
  performance, 136–7
  standards, 137
Marketing and production, 126
MacClelland, 14
MacKinsey, 109n1
MacMahon, J. T., 13n51
McMillan, C., 13, 20n23

Measurement of performance and evolution, 138
Missing link between comparative, 14
Mouton and Blake, 14
Multinational behaviour abroad, 16
Myers, C. A., 10, 12, 19n3, 20n16, 154, 161n7

Nath, R., 11, 20n9
Negandhi, A. R., 11, 13, 19n6, 20n21, 21n36, 181n25
Newman, W. H., 28n8, 32, 33, 37n22, 37n29, 175n7
Nowothny, 154n5

Oberg, W., 13, 20n22
Objectives, 93, 106, 122–4, 151, 153, 154, 186
  influence of, 32
  of control, 87, 106
  of the study, 5
O'Donnell, 171
Operation control, 126, 144, 153–9, 167–8, 171
  check on subordinates decisions, 131, 136
  critical for evaluation of performance, 130–1
  frequency, 131
  information, 124
  level, 54, 152–7, 163
  matters, 79, 103
  marketing, 138
  production, 139
  use of rules, 131
Organisation of the book, 4
Organisation of planning, 72
Owner entrepreneur versus professional management, 155

Perlmutter, H. U., 16, 22n40
Perrow, C., 32, 37n18, 178, 184n19
Philipps, 17n48
Pitts, J. R., 158n17
Planning, 90, 102, 144–7, 156–9, 166, 170, 173, 174, 175, 180, 186, 187, 188, 189
  and structure, 53
  content, 72, 167

cycle, 122
director, 67
influence of controller on, 123
manual, 70–4
process, 75–9, 122, 149
short range, 77, 82, 116, 122, 179
Process of organising, 54
Process-Oriented studies, 16
Production, 59, 76, 90–6, 104, 118, 121–2, 133, 150, 153, 159, 165, 187–8
control, 125, 131, 138, 139, 140, 143, 144, 156–7, 171, 186
director, 49
Formalism, 130
Managers, 46
Objectives, 135
Performance, 139, 140
Standards, 140
units, 109, 177
Professional managers, 155–9, 188–9
Professionalisation, 149, 175
Profit
accounting, 114, 116
centres, 116, 117, 119, 186
Pugh, D. S., 178, 184n15

Rate
of change, 32, 172
of inflation, 151
Rationalisation, 155, 169
Report, 54, 84, 95, 98, 119, 123–5
to chief executives, 94, 98, 114, 117
qualitative, 98
Research
basic design, 38
design and methodology, 5
previous, 58
strategy of, 24
Richman, B. M., 13, 14, 20n20, 21n27
Roberts, K. H., 11, 19n8
Robock, S. H., 13, 20n19
Rostow, W. W., 11n13
Rumelt, R. P., 58n3
Rutenberg, D. P., 16, 22n44

Savage, D., 159, 161n20, 176, 183n8
Schöllhammer, H., 10, 11, 14n30, 19n5, 20n11
Scope of study, 3
of field, 1
Score, 67
Scott, B. R., 32, 37n26, 58n2, 179, 184n20
Sehti, S. P., 13
Sherman, 31n16
Sirota, D., 16n48
Staff, 44, 54–5, 65–6, 84, 115, 121–2, 137, 173
and line, 65
central, 65, 94, 115, 148, 187
function, 105
Stahl, W., 156n11
Standard, 71–6, 82, 116, 133, 135, 136, 137, 140–3, 181
Standardisation, 114
Statistical scanning, 163
Steering control, 175
Steiner, G. A., 26
Stopford, J., 9n2
Strategy, 23, 148, 188
Structural, 172
arrangements, 84
characterististics, 70
differences, 69
interpretation, 106
Structure, 78, 118, 144–9, 153, 166, 170, 173, 178, 179
divisional, 59, 61–2, 116, 167
functional, 59, 61, 111, 167
holding, 54, 171
product-market, 56–8, 108, 162, 189
Systematisation, 104, 114

Tannenbaum, A. S., 25n5
Taylor, F. W., 31, 36n11
Technology, 177
Thiagarangan, 17
Tightness of grasp, 132
Top management, 103, 105, 114, 117–19, 123–4, 143, 153–4 163–7, 174, 176
committee, 68, 87
control, 90, 93

Top managerial
  control effectiveness, 101
  level, 26, 88
  manager's report, 93
  team, 63
Trepo, G. X., 158n17

Variables, 30, 119
  business, 30, 32
  country, 34
  management system, 33
Vernon, R., 16, 22n42

Vorstand, 45, 59, 64–8, 111–12, 158

Wallich, H. C., 154
Warner and Abegglen, 197
Webber, R. A., 13, 20n19, 172
Weinschall, T. D., 35n36, 157n12, 158
Woodward, J., 32, 37n17, 178, 184n16
Wrapp, H. E., 34n32
Wrigley, L., 58n1

Zenoff, D. B., 16, 22n43
Zwick, J., 16, 22n43